A CEO's Secret Weapon
By Frumi Rachel Barr, Ph.D.

Book description

How many leaders truly know their cause and purpose in life and pursue it with a passion that makes others envious? Few. How many of those leaders translate that passion into their enterprise? Fewer still. Readers of *A CEO's Secret Weapon* discover how to do exactly that.

Frumi Barr employs the theory of projecting your inner self into the company. She harnesses the power of knowing your *Why* to implement solutions that work. Says Frumi, "Harness your inner passion—whatever it is—to become the most committed advocate for your cause that ever existed." With the help of *A CEO's Secret Weapon*, that is a realistic goal.

The book accomplishes this objective in 10 powerful chapters; each shining a bright light on the most potentially disruptive and destructive issues facing business leaders and CEOs every day. Frumi deconstructs each, then shows just how to navigate around the rocks and shoals that can punch a hole in the hull. Chapter 4, "High Stakes Conversations", for example, shows how anyone can harness dissention and turn it to their advantage. Have an aggressive subordinate? Want to turn that aggression into a productively assertive leader? Read on. Indeed, *High Stakes Conversations* leaves nothing to chance that could derail the success you deserve. Frumi shows you how. The other 9 chapters are just as essential and produce the same phenomenal results.

But wait. There's more. The book uses case studies to illustrate ways to best implement the Leader's passion for their cause, purpose and *Why*. Peppered throughout the book are: CEO's real life examples of the most confounding issues they face and what they did about them. Some succeeded, some didn't. Frumi dissects what went right and what they could have done to achieve a different outcome.

A CEO's Secret Weapon is 51,000 words of extraordinary commentary about what's bugging today's leaders and what they can do about it. Certainly, CEOs need to know what Frumi Rachel Barr says in this book. Along with business, the same issues confront leaders of most organizations, be it nonprofits, military, government, religious organizations or others. Leading and managing is a contact sport. Whether you lead a combat fighter squadron or a group of CPAs, sooner or later you'll need to strengthen your team's cohesiveness (Chapter 7, "Making Your Why Come Alive") in the face of new challenges. Frumi shows you how.

Dr. Barr walks the talk. She has been the CEO of three enterprises and the CFO of two others. She has an MBA and a Ph.D. as well as multiple certifications in related specialties. She serves as personal confidante and coach to a number of high-profile CEOs. Dr. Barr is in the management trenches every working day.

Read and study *A CEO's Secret Weapon*. Harness your personal power that comes from knowing your own cause, purpose and *Why*. Then use the passion that comes with that knowledge to realize your organization's fullest potential. Don't wait another minute. Achieving your most complete personal success is just 10 short chapters away.

* * *

Dedication

To Soldier Sam, an incredible man who I had the honor of calling Daddy. He made his final journey May 8th, 2012 with his family (including me and my own children) at his bedside in Montreal.

The paradox was that this gentle man survived World War II after being in the first of the Special Forces, a joint US and Canadian force. He was the first Jewish Canadian paratrooper barely making it over the 5'5" height limit. Of the 1800 men who joined the force, over 1400 never returned from battle. By the grace of God my Daddy was one of those who returned.

He was a wonderful husband, father, grandfather, and an Entrepreneur. He would have loved to have this book when he started on his entrepreneurial adventure. I learned a lot form his perseverance and can do attitude.

November 16, 1914 to May 8, 2012

A CEO's Secret Weapon

By Frumi Rachel Bar

Published by Frumi Barr at Smashwords
All rights reserved
Copyright 2012 by Frumi Barr
Smashwords Edition
This eBook is licensed for your personal use and enjoyment only. This eBook may not be re-sold or given away to others. If you would like to share this book, please purchase an additional copy for each recipient. If you are reading this book and did not purchase it, or it was not purchased for your use only, then please return to Smashwords.com and purchase your own copy. Thank you for respecting the hard work of the author.

Library of Congress Cataloging-in-Publication Data
Barr, Frumi
A CEO's Secret Weapon / Frumi Barr
ISBN 9781479337934
1. Discovering your Why. 2. High stakes conversations. 3. Talking about what matters. 4. Assemble your WHO's. 5. The power of Why.

Table of Content

Foreword

Preface

Chapter 1: Discovering Your WHY: An Inside Job 1

Chapter 2: Good Times or Bad, You're Still the CEO 21

Chapter 3: Iceberg, Dead Ahead! 39

Chapter 4: High Stakes Conversations: Talking About What Matters 59

Chapter 5: Staying Positive under Fire: What are you thinking? 80

Chapter 6: Assemble Your WHOs: Tapping Resources 102

Chapter 7: Implementing: Making Your WHY Come Alive 115

Chapter 8: Growing the enterprise 130

Chapter 9: The Power of Why 146

Chapter 10: Becoming the Leader Others Want to Follow .. 167

About the author 178

Connect with me online 178

See My Products 178

A final word from the author 178

The Why Institute 180

CEO Virtual Roundtables... 183

Foreword

To be a leader you only need one thing and one thing only: Followers. That's it. A follower is someone who raises his or her hand and chooses to go in the direction you point. They volunteer to work to help advance towards the vision or destination the leader lays out. Often they will do it at personal sacrifice. Not because they were asked to, but because they choose to.

Authority can get people to do things. However, having authority does not make someone a leader. A leader is only a leader when others choose to follow. The question is, why should anyone follow you?

I have learned that the great leaders—those with the capacity to inspire others to act, everyone from Martin Luther King, Jr. to Steve Jobs all think, act and communicate the exact same way…and it's the complete opposite to the rest of us. What I have learned is that they all start with Why—the purpose, cause or belief that drives us. A clear sense of Why you do what you do is like an internal compass. No matter in which direction you face, that compass does not change the way it faces. And just as having a compass is the only way to navigate out of the woods or reach a chosen destination, so too is a clear sense of Why the only way to navigate through hard times or build a vision.

Frumi Barr is one of those bright lights who joined me in this cause that I have to inspire people to do what inspires them. To help build a vision of a world in which the vast majority of people wake up every single day inspired to go to work and return home fulfilled by the work they do.

Without an clichés or psychobabble, Frumi found her own style to guide leaders who inspire or who have the potential to inspire their own Why—to get a clear sense of the fixed point to which their compass points. More valuable, she teaches those leaders to navigate with that compass. To use their Why to build organizations, make decisions and decide on strategies that help

A CEO's Secret Weapon

advance their cause—to help them reach the destination they imagine.

In the few years that I have known Frumi she has inspired me with her undying conviction. Her undying belief in people. Her want to do good in the world. Her complete selflessness. I love that she has written her own book to share her ideas with even more people. I know the more people who learn these ideas, the greater the chance we have to build that world I imagine. A world in which we are inspired and fulfilled by the work we do.

Thank you to Frumi for being a part of this movement and good luck to all of you who are about to continue on your journey with a remarkable guide by your side.

Inspire on!

Simon Sinek

Preface

The CEO of any enterprise has a tough job. Think about it. They make all the decisions and champion the cause all the way to success. The CEO bears the blame for all failures. The boss sets the priorities for everyone working at the enterprise. All crises land on the CEO's doorstep—most are urgent, potentially catastrophic affairs.

What happens when the CEO does things right and the enterprise succeeds? The chief humbly stands aside and turns over all credit to the team who made it happen. After all, positively motivating the team always trumps the CEO's own emotional needs. The team's collective ego demands constant feeding. Both tasks fall on the CEO's shoulders.

CEOs live on a high wire, balancing between making their company successful and achieving the profit imperative while deploying scarce assets in the most strategically advantageous ways. The CEO has no one to act as a mentor; no sage guru from whom to seek advice.

Therein lies the challenge of being the boss. I discovered this truth during my tenure as the CEO of three different companies. At no time did I have a coach or an all-knowing mentor. Yet the buck always crashed onto my desk, skidding to a stop right there in my lap. The crises never went away until *I* made them go away. Now I mentor a number of CEOs. I'm still in the trenches, but have a complete view of life within the beast.

A CEO's Secret Weapon represents a career's worth of identifying common problems, and then finding the solutions facing the occupant of every corner office. While researching this book I interviewed 40 CEOs of every size enterprise imaginable. I grew to know each one and still stay in touch. They all confirmed what I had experienced—it is indeed lonely at the top. No surprise there. But what is surprising is how hungry they are for someone to talk to about the non-technical, softer issues they face every day. These are the very issues that launch companies to the top of their industries and their CEOs along with them.

Not just anyone will do, though. It has to be someone who has walked in their shoes; someone who has experienced life on the firing line. Funny thing, every CEO I interviewed was eager to receive a copy of this book just as soon as it was done.

Why the urgency to read this book? What did these seasoned business leaders see in my premise? The answer is hiding in plain sight. It is now, always has been, and forever will be within each of us unique individuals. *A CEO's Secret Weapon is everything you were never taught in biz school—it's here so you can learn from others' mistakes.* No psychobabble here. After all, this is a business book written for seasoned, time-constrained executives.

You will discover why you do what you do (Chapter 1: "An Inside Job") and how that behavior manifests itself into your company's and subordinates' performance. The most important words in this book—*Why, How, What and Who*—are words you will come to know, but in a way you never expected and presented within a business context designed to be immediately useful in your business life today (Chapter 2: "You're Still the CEO" and Chapter 3: "Weathering the Storm"). *Why, How, What and Who.* These four simple words will become your most powerful allies and most devastating competitive weapons.

Among the tools in this book, you'll actually see how to unearth what really matters (Chapter 4: "High Stakes Conversations") in those exchanges that disrupt the strategic balance of entire industries and enterprises along with the lives of everyone working there. You will learn how to look within to remain calm and objective during conflict (Chapter 5: "Staying Positive Under Fire").

By design, when readers finish *A CEO's Secret Weapon* they can quickly marshal decision-making assets (Chapter 6: "Assembling the Who's"). The emphasis here is not just on the theory of projecting your inner self into the company, but also on implementing real world solutions that work (Chapter 7: "Making Your Why Come Alive"). My intent is to harness your inner passion—whatever it is—to become the most committed advocate for your cause that ever existed (Chapter 8: "Growing the Enterprise").

Even with these tools at the ready, you would be surprised to know how many otherwise accomplished CEOs actually sabotage their own agendas. After reading Chapter 9: "Gaining and Maintaining Power as a CEO", you will prevent this from happening to you.

How to use the book

Each chapter presents challenges to the CEO. The typical push back is, "I've been there before. I know what I did. I saw the resulting successes and shortcomings." Instead, you'll see some alternative approaches coming from another direction and learn how to use them as extraordinarily effective management tools. In that sense, *A CEO's Secret Weapon* is a reference book.

If you aren't facing the challenges shown in each chapter today, I promise that you will face them tomorrow. This is the reason to read the entire book in sequence. Forewarned is forearmed.

I hope you enjoy reading the lessons that I had to learn the hard way in *A CEO's Secret Weapon*. As the author, I want this book to make a difference in the way you harness the incredible energy and resources locked away inside of you. Once you understand your *Why*, the *How, the What* and the *Who*, there is no stopping you. You have a date with destiny. Let's arrange the meeting. I invite you to come along and join me on the most incredible journey—I promise it will change your life and career forever.

Let's roll,

Frumi Rachel Barr

Chapter 1: Discovering Your WHY: An Inside Job

Conflict—it's a word that drips with negativity—adversaries, risk, possible defeat and dire consequences, the list goes on. Conflict is what keeps the boss awake at night. The top two conflicts are competing financial needs and incompatible priorities. Yours may be different. Still, the point is that every conflict is urgent. Each choice means foregoing something else with equal merit. Conflict grinds the CEO's decision mechanism to a stop like sand thrown into well-oiled gears.

What would you say if I told you that there's a way to shield those well-oiled gears of decision making from the grinding sand of conflict? Would you want to hear how to do that? Of course you would. The answer lies in *Why*. Here's what I mean.

Finding the power of Why

Social psychologists urge their followers to find their inner selves. It's a pop mantra that we won't chant. Instead, we define your *Why* as something very specific. It is your most valuable business tool. Knowing your *Why* is the first step. *Why* is simply understanding, accepting and articulating your own purpose and that of your enterprise. Think of it as a guide.

Don't confuse *Why* with *How* and *What*. *Why* is simply your purpose, your cause and your belief. It is essentially, *Why* you are here. *What*, on the other hand, is what you do. It's easily identifiable. If you are the CEO of Ford, *What* is that you make cars. If you are IBM, you make computers. *How* is only slightly less readily identified. *How* is your guiding values and the process by which you create your result. It is your manufacturing process, your patents, your factories and your employees.

But we're after your *Why*—a more difficult, introspective task to identify. Think of your purpose in life and that of your enterprise.

What is your cause? What do you believe in? For example, Michael Kobold founded the Kobold Watch Company just 15 years ago (a newbie by watch industry standards). Here's Mike's *Why*:

"Embrace Adventure. This short phrase is Kobold's battle cry that reminds us what Kobold watches are all about—the pursuit of adventure. This distinguishes us from the competition and tells our unique story. At Kobold, it's a story we live everyday. That is why, with our brand ambassadors—British explorer Sir Ranulph Fienens and mountain guide Kenton Cool—the men and women of the Kobold Watch Company have tackled a number of adventures themselves. This authenticity filters through our watches—without a doubt the toughest in the industry."

—Michael Kobold, CEO, Kobold Watch Company, Pittsburgh, PA

Such purpose comes from deep within. It is authentic. People see that honesty. They trust the man with the fortitude to reveal it in public. Kobold's employees work there for money, yes, but also because their own purpose and beliefs strongly parallel the boss's. Customers see that too. Kobold's watches go not just to those whose lives often depend on the information they provide but also to those who resonate with and share the boss's insistence on precision and durability. Essentially, Kobold's employees and customers share his own cause of uncompromising precision, strength and endurance. They share his *Why*.

Here's another *Why*—it is that of the company I head:

"The Why Institute inspires leaders to shape their future, take decisive action and sustain momentum to build sustainable companies. The Why Institute provides a safe environment for them to do so. Leaders have the conversations that really

matter—the beginning of discovering and implementing their own Why."

—Dr. Frumi Barr, Ph.D., CEO of The Why Institute, Newport Beach, CA

When you think about why you do what you do, go a little deeper than just the obvious. Some will say, "We do what we do to make money." That's only the most superficial reason—and not a very good reason at that. You can make money anywhere, doing most anything. Don't let go of the question until you've plumbed the depths of your purpose, your cause and how your personal beliefs drive the enterprise. You know you've hit on your *Why* when you can say, "This is my function; it is what I stand for; my company exists for these things. It is the first, last and the only reason we endure."

Other examples of Why

Successful enterprises, and the CEOs who run them, have a firm grip on why they exist; everything they do and every decision they make must meet that standard. These CEOs lead from the inside out. For example, they might state their beliefs and commitment to a clean, germ-free environment that is healthy and reduces people's chance of illness. It just so happens that they make soap. Want to buy some?

Apple Computer

Apple is without a doubt an extraordinary company. Its co-founder, Steve Jobs, was an extraordinary individual. He was indeed the face of Apple as well as its driving force. What was Jobs' advantage? What did he have that Dell, IBM, Microsoft and the long defunct Atari didn't?

It wasn't talent. Apple hired from the same employee pool to which every other computer manufacturer had access. Jobs had available to him the very same consultants as his competitors. He also used the same print and broadcast advertising media as everyone else.

Was Apple somehow not subject to the same laws of physics and electronics as the others? Certainly not. What then? What did Jobs do differently after he was reappointed CEO?

Before he left to start Pixar and his other ventures, Apple told customers the same thing every competitor said: "We make great computers. We design them well. They are easy to use and user friendly. Want to buy one?"

This outside-in orientation focused on the *What.* That is, the product. It pitted Apple against everyone else and tried to better them in a head-to-head competition of features. There was no differentiation. Every computer manufacturer had access to the same components, engineering talents and managers. Apple was on a slippery slope, sliding toward oblivion.

When Steve Jobs returned to retake Apple's helm, he brought with him a most deadly competitive weapon—he understood *Why.* Jobs reoriented Apple from focusing on merely the product. He changed the cause to an imperative he had found within himself during his hiatus. If those around him shared this belief they could climb aboard. If not, then Apple was no longer the place for them.

Jobs' *Why* probably went something like this:

We choose to challenge an industry that is choking on its own arrogant inability to listen to customers and create the innovations they want and need. We face this challenge in all that we undertake. We choose to think differently. We make beautifully designed products that emphasize functionality based on a friendly, helpful relationship with our users. We are here to make life easier for everyone using connected technology. We happen to make great computers. Can we make one for you?

With that clarity of purpose, Jobs was suddenly communicating authentically. Once you get it, you'll communicate like Steve Jobs too. The picture of your life and business opens. Your purpose—the *Why*—becomes your gold standard against which you measure all life and business decisions. You'll see the results of this awakening almost immediately.

Southwest Airlines is the perfect example of a company that makes decisions based on their Why (to put people in the air safely and at a cost below any other airline). An employee once suggested serving a high-end, costly Caesar salad aboard flights to raise the company's stature. The answer was a quick and resounding "NO!" This suggestion was not in alignment with the company's Why—its reason for existence.

Manifestations of knowing Why

Once you've identified why you and your company are here, your reason for being, and your purpose, you'll see some changes. First, people will more readily listen to you. Unlike most others, you now speak from a concrete conviction that emanates from deep within you. Such unshakable belief in oneself—especially when others don't have it—translates into credibility. People can see that you have something they don't. They actively seek out the opinion of such savants.

Once you have found your reason for being and your cause, you'll see how easy it is to be totally honest and authentic with people. In my role as mentor and advisor to CEOs, I see many who only play the role of being honest and concerned. They think, say and act according to what they think the company line demands of them. Few believe it.

An example is the hapless Tony Hayward, former CEO of British Petroleum. Shortly after the company's oilrig, Deep Water Horizon, went down killing 11 and horribly polluting the Gulf, it became apparent where Hayward's cause really lay. It was not in righting the terrible wrong of repeated safety violations. It was obvious that Hayward and BP shared a culture of placing profit performance ahead of people's needs.

Hayward's arrogance ruined millions of people's lives for a significant time. His first honest quote came on June 1, 2010 when he said, *"...There's no one who wants this over more than I do. I'd like my life back."* Yes, Tony. So would the millions whose lives you damaged.

The postscript to British Petroleum is that they fired Hayward. The company board carefully selected his replacement more for his political correctness than anything else. Bob Dudley, a native of Mississippi, came out speaking of growing up on the Gulf Coast, and cherishing the time he'd spent swimming in Gulf waters. He said these things even while the company he headed was challenging the safety violations OSHA continued bringing against the company he headed. See the disconnect? Here is a company that does one thing—pursue the bottom line regardless of the consequences to their employees and the public—while saying something quite different to the world community and trying to make everyone believe it.

Of course, people will continue to work for BP. However, their motivation is for a paycheck. This is a far weaker commitment than those who share the CEO's cause, and believe it is worthwhile and good. These people believe in something far bigger than themselves. Speaking from the heart suddenly comes naturally, without pretense or contrivance. There's no worry about what others may think, though they may not necessarily like what you say, they'll still listen.

Former President George W. Bush stated this very clearly right after the attacks of 911. Before a joint session of Congress on September 20, 2001, President Bush said, "Either you are with us or you are with the terrorists." Our President had suddenly found his *Why*. There is no doubt that he spoke from the heart.

For those who believe in a clear purpose and feel a true sense of fulfillment, work becomes fun and they can't wait to start the day. Their work becomes their passion because what they do is so closely aligned with who they are.

The Culture starts with YOU

Good leaders knock down obstacles impairing their people's success. They lead by example. If they exhibit a good example, their people will likely share that behavior. The same thing holds for a CEO who exhibits behavior contrary to the organization's purpose and cause.

Two individuals owned a billion dollar distributor of consumer electronics. The company's purpose was to speed necessary products from the manufacturer to the point of sale in a precise, low cost way. This was the Chief Operating Officer's purpose. It was his cause and it translated to all who worked for him. The COO loved his job and was good at it. He not only got a lot done, but was deeply respected by his subordinates, the company's vendors and its customers.

The CEO had a different story entirely. The CEO owned 51 percent of the company. He resented the COO's popularity and the respect he had earned. As a result, the CEO came in late and left early. By default, the COO had to take over most of the CEO's responsibilities since he was so seldom there when critical decisions needed to be made. The CEO merely mouthed the company's purpose and mission. But he was transparent. People saw right through his lack of authenticity. Soon the COO stopped inviting him to vendor and customer meetings and the employees ceased seeking his advice. A war erupted between both owners. The company went down fast, and soon was on the brink of going under. The CEO almost lost a once extraordinarily prosperous enterprise because he was living in conflict with his organization's reason for being—an organization he co-founded and helped build.

Changing the culture

We all know that an organization's culture and its agenda come from the top. Everything the CEO does influences the way the enterprise operates. Steve Jobs marched back into Apple's executive offices with a new idea and a new purpose. He realized that his first challenge was to change Apple's culture into one that cared, listened to and acted upon its customer's needs and desires. How do you do that?

First, you take some time to inventory the cultural traits of the organization as it is currently. Then see how those characteristics stack up against what the company needs to have in order to meet its new purpose, vision and cause. From this assessment, you'll see what parts of the old culture can still be used and should be nurtured through the restructuring. Dismiss the rest.

Too often people think they have no ability to change anything in their company, let alone something so fundamentally all consuming as its mission and cause. In order to do this, you must take the next step—surround yourself with your organization's change agents. These people have the ability, respect and following to effect change. They may not necessarily be your senior executives. Dig into the organization and seek out these people. Bring them into your confidence and share your cause and vision. Chances are, these individuals have already recognized that the enterprise needs a change. Most respond to the CEO sharing their *Why*, their cause and their reason. In many cases, it won't take much convincing that your deep-seated belief in these changes is the best chance for creating something extraordinary.

Implementing necessary changes

Now you know what changes to make. You have assembled the organization's change agents capable of implementing the necessary conversions. What now, Mr. CEO?

Assemble your team. Take them completely into your confidence as anything less creates a cloud of distrust and inauthenticity. Guide them in understanding the incredible effects their own behavior can have on the culture of the organization.

Many CEOs treat this as what it is—a culture changing project. With their team, they identify what cultural changes the enterprise needs. They assign champions who the group holds accountable for making specific changes. There is no punishment or penalty for failing. Each change agent (or champion) already supports the cause and is a committed member of the team. They may indeed fail in completing their assigned task, but it won't be for lack of trying. Further, the change group will help and support them because everyone shares the same mission and cause. If one thing doesn't work, then another direction just might. When Steve Jobs turned around Apple, it wasn't a smooth road. There were lots of trials and errors; some came from within the organization and many came from vendors, distributors and the customers themselves.

The role of self-awareness and self-reflection

Once you've found your *Why*—your cause and reason for being—how do you sell it? It's surprisingly easy. Authenticity and belief in what you're doing comes through in everything you do. People see that. They trust such passion for a cause. Where people may have a hard time buying *what* you do, they have no problem joining you in *why* you do it.

Remember earlier we guessed at Apple's cause: *To disrupt the status quo by thinking differently. We just happen to make computers.* This came from Steve Jobs after a period of self-reflection. He returned to the company and brought with him a deep self-awareness and, of course, his cause for connecting people with the user-friendly technology they wanted and needed. We found the same thing to be true of Michael Kobold's cause: *Embrace adventure…it's a story we live every day…this authenticity filters through our watches.*

There are true leaders and then there are those with the mere title of leader. These people sit in the C-suite and rule what they sometimes think is their kingdom. It is not. Every day they must prove themselves worthy of trust from their board, their investors and the employees, all of whom they serve.

True leaders know what got them to the top. They never forget it. Their motivations come from a cause and purpose in which they truly believe. Their enthusiasm and commitment is contagious to those around them. They surround themselves with people to whom this resonates.

True leaders are aware of this mechanism. They are self-aware and unafraid of self-reflection. There is nothing to hide from themselves or from others. They hold themselves accountable for furthering their cause and living their *Why*.

Knowing these things about you and your company allows you to better execute the job of CEO. It's easier to talk with customers and employees. Leadership gets easier too. All results in better decisions.

Sam Langley vs. Orville & Wilbur Wright

History is replete with tales of those who rejected the accolades of personal achievement and instead pursued a higher cause that benefited others. A good example is the infamous Samuel Pierpont Langley who lived between 1834 and 1906. Langley sold the War Department and the Smithsonian Institution on giving him $100,000 (a huge sum in those days) to research and create a flying machine that carried a pilot. So caught up in his quest for personal fame and fortune, Langley wasn't even aware that the Wright brothers existed.

Langley had all the credentials for success: He was highly educated, had a huge wad of cash to spend, and his stature as Secretary of the Smithsonian Institution lent him great credibility. Indeed, he was not without some success in flying. Langley built an unmanned aerodrome (his sixth attempt) that flew 4,200 feet at about 30 mph on November 28, 1896. There was no way to steer this craft even if it had a pilot, which it did not. There were others working on the same project elsewhere around the world.

Langley felt the hot breath of competition to be the first to develop a manned aircraft that flew. He thought his best chance to beat his competitors and gain the fame and fortune he so desperately sought, was to catapult his aircraft into the sky from a boat on the Potomac River. Half of his funds went to building this launch boat.

Langley's drive to be first clouded his judgment. He refused to listen to those who pointed out the perils of a water launch and developing what amounted to the first aircraft carrier. His ego caused him to ignore the two brothers who owned a bicycle shop.

The shop provided just $1,000 for the materials the Wright brothers needed to build their airplane. Their cause was not to gain fame and riches. The Wrights just wanted to launch the world into the air, navigate around awhile, and then land safely. That's all. Fame and fortune versus the miracle of manned flight. Between Langley's goal and the Wright's, which was the more difficult feat?

Langley's fragile wood and fabric airplane, really no stronger than a large kite, had to go from a dead stop to 60 mph in just 70 feet. The stress of the catapult launch was more than his flimsy craft could withstand. The launch so badly damaged the plane that it crashed right off of the catapult. Witnesses said the aircraft flew like a handful of mortar. Even worse, Langley's pilot (not him, how is that for commitment?) nearly drowned in the icy Potomac River.

Just eight days after Langley's crash, the Wright's sturdy little aircraft clawed its way into the air at Kitty Hawk. They had mastered manned flight for the first time. There were no photographers or reporters to capture the very first flight. Indeed, the world didn't find out about the Wright's success until several days after it happened. The Wrights worked not for fame or riches. They worked because they had found their purpose and their cause.

Langley died in 1906, a broken and bitterly disappointed man. The truth is, he had never taken an introspective look at why he was here and doing what he was doing. Even if he had succeeded, flew his airplane and become rich and famous, he still would have seen himself as having failed. For such a shallow purpose as Langley's, there will always be others richer and more famous. He was like a hamster on a treadmill to nowhere. The Wright brothers, on the other hand, were committed to a cause much

A CEO's Secret Weapon

greater than themselves. They were first. However, my guess is that being first was of little consequence to them. Mankind had finally broken his earthly bonds—that was what probably excited them.

Thinking from the inside out

Great leaders think and communicate the opposite way others do. Great leaders communicate from the inside out. They talk of their passion. It ties directly with what they're doing. They purposefully joined both their cause and their life's work. They get others to sign on with them because of *Why* they're doing what they do. Their truth and sincerity resonates with others. Leaders let people look inside themselves. People see what's there and they trust that there is no hidden agenda.

After all of the quantitative analysis of financial forecasts and marketing assessments, at the end of the day all major decisions come from the heart, not the brain. Have you ever heard a CEO listen to compelling analyses providing incontrovertible mathematical proof of a decision? Then the CEO shakes his head and says, "Sorry. It just doesn't *feel* right." Or, "No, this doesn't *pass the smell test*." Neither comment has anything to do with logic or the brain's decision-making capabilities. Instead, it has to do with the heart. That's what CEOs are paid to do. Their boards and investors trust their heart and gut instincts over quantitative assumptions.

If we accept that people's most compelling decisions come not from the brain, but from the heart, then the goal of marketing is not to sell people on what you have. Rather, it is to sell them on what you believe. Apple says the entire company exists to make life easier for everyone using connected technology; that is how they think differently. Apple is selling a cause, not a computer. Those who sign on with Apple's cause will support them. It just so happens that Apple makes computers and other high-tech

13

communications devices. Buying their products is a gesture of support and agreement with that cause. Those early adopters who stand in line for hours and hours just to be the first to get the latest iPhone do it because they believe in Apple's cause and want to be a part of it. They are making a powerful statement of their individuality.

Not thinking from the inside out

Do you remember the original digital video recorder? It was the TiVo. This company's fate is the classic solution in search of a problem to solve. The engineers at TiVo had developed a cool technology that stopped live television, paused it, recorded it and allowed viewers to skip ahead in prescribed chunks to avoid commercials.

That was TiVo's solution. But what was the problem they were solving? They didn't know. Don't forget, the video tape recorder did many of these things too, but in a clumsier, mechanical, non-digital way. At first, customers didn't believe TiVo's advertising claims, nor could they see what advantage the TiVo machine gave them over the VCR. Then there was the value proposition. The VCR was a single cash outlay. TiVo, however, required you to sign up for a monthly service plan in addition to buying (or in some cases, renting) the TiVo machine.

TiVo was selling *what* they did. Their pitch was, "Here's a cool technology that stops live television, pauses it, records it and allows you to skip commercials. Want to buy one?" This is a pitch from the outside—what they do. It didn't work. The company's stock plummeted.

Instead, they should have clearly defined their purpose for existing—to provide people greater control over their valuable leisure time—and pitched that. This would have been speaking from the inside, out. Indeed, the modern DVR is about control and convenience. That's the message that resonates.

The dream of a great man

Martin Luther King was a great orator, with a spectacular message. Back then, there were many equally gifted speakers with similar messages. What did King have that the others lacked? How could a Baptist minister, born in Atlanta, draw stadium-sized crowds with little or no advance marketing? His gift was that he *believed*. His cause and purpose was to end racial segregation and discrimination through civil disobedience and other nonviolent means. King wasn't shy about telling people his dream of equality. His total honesty and transparency drew people to him. They took his belief and made it their own. They showed up at his rallies because they believed in the dream too. It just so happened that King shared *their* beliefs.

True leaders inspire people. Their followers aspire to share their beliefs. They want to follow such a leader for themselves. It's a much more powerful motivation—this leading from the inside out.

Sharing your vision

Those with a tightly focused cause and purpose have a vision. They don't seek to cram it down anyone's throat. Instead, their passion and enthusiasm attracts others. It soon becomes a common vision shared among many.

A good example is Tony Hsieh (pronounced, Shay). Hsieh was already a wealthy man (having sold his startup, LinkExchange, to Microsoft for $265 million). Nick Swinmurn asked him to invest in his online shoe store, ShoeSite.com. Hsieh and his Venture Frogs partner, Alfred Lin, put up $500,000. They changed the company's name to a snappier, Zappos.com (a variation on *zapatos* in Spanish, meaning shoes). They had just three very simple goals. One was to bring great customer service—they just happened to sell shoes at an affordable price. Another was to hit $1 billion in sales by 2010. The third was to become one of the best places to work in the country.

Hsieh built Zappos completely around customer service, which started with happy, committed employees—that was his purpose. This purpose required complete control over the customer experience. They made the stomach-churning decision to stop drop-shipping product, costing them 25 percent of their 2003 sales. They did it because drop shipments removed their control of the customer experience. Since their purpose was to provide a great customer experience, this decision was one that they felt compelled to make.

By 2008 Zappos hit Hsieh's second goal, $1 billion in sales. The next year, Hsieh hit his third goal, entering Fortune's list of "Top 100 Companies To Work For", by debuting all the way up at number 23. Amazon purchased Zappos in 2009 for $1.2 billion.

Transparent motivations

The story of Tony Hsieh is rare, but not necessarily unique among ultra-successful, employee/customer-oriented companies. Facebook is reputed to have such a corporate culture. The reason these enterprises treat their people and customers so well is because it is a key part of their purpose.

However, some companies do their employees favors for the wrong reasons and it bites them in the behind. The securities firm, Donaldson Lufkin Jenrette (bought by Credit Suisse in 2000) is a good example. The company had a policy of feeding their employees. There would be lavish breakfast and lunch buffets every day, and sometimes dinner too. They provided valets who ran errands for which the big producers didn't have time.

However, the message was clear even though it was subtly communicated. These perks are here because we want you to work harder to make us more money. Profit is our cause and our purpose. Employees and customers are just an unavoidable evil we put up with to get us the money.

DLJ's employees hated the company. Many jumped ship at the first chance they got. They felt no link or affinity to the company like Hsieh's employees. The result is that DLJ was absorbed and Zappos is still flourishing in the Amazon environment. Zappos believes in *delivering happiness*. DLJ was a money grab. Which is the enduring model?

Communicating from the inside out

This is an art form. However, it is a *learnable* art form. People listen to leaders and allow them to lead only if the speaker believes in himself and what he is saying. Being authentic (as Tony Hsieh was and DLJ was not) is essential. Those with a firm grip on their *Why*—their purpose and cause—are not afraid of pushback. Try it. Challenge such a person on why they do what they do. Most will respond from a deep inner conviction. They don't sell, they simply explain something that is crystal clear to them and that they believe is worth pursuing. You can see their actions tie directly with their cause.

Now, try pushing back to someone without such a cause and commitment. You are in for a fight. Their argument will center on the *what*—the outcome and things, performance and products. They say things like, "How can you argue with success?" Of course, they are the ones who define success.

Step 1: Communicating authentically

Communicating from the inside out requires you to be authentic. Drop the hidden agenda. Find your cause—your *why*. Become aware of yourself and your motives and how you got to where you are now. Keep what ties in with your purpose and disengage yourself from the rest. Recall that Zappos made the decision to eliminate 25 percent of their total 2003 revenue because they couldn't control the customer's experience using drop shipments. This was a very expensive decision. It was authentic because it tied directly to the company's purpose and core belief of giving customers a great experience.

Step 2: Understand your motives

Take inventory of the actions you took to get to your current station in life and business. Identify how you did it. From such introspective research comes understanding of what you're going to change and what new things you will do that conform to your purpose and your destination. Step 2 provides the mechanism of change.

However, change is not yet implemented. Often people don't know how to implement change. Sometimes they still need to surround themselves with the right team or resources. For some there is a fear of failure that renders them immobile. They believe the devil you know is better than the devil you don't.

For others there is the fear of success. Imagine a professional golfer who often leads the tournament right until the last few holes, then blows up and comes in a consistent second. The reason? The winner has to be interviewed on television and must give a speech. The golfer was deathly afraid of public speaking. That was Annika Sorenstam during her younger years on the LPGA tour. Once she got over her fear of success, she won 72 official LPGA tournaments including 10 majors and 18 other tournaments internationally. Sorenstam tops the LPGA's career money list.

Step 3: Implementing your Why

At this stage, you're communicating authentically. You have a newfound mental clarity. The picture of your life and business is clear. You have found your *Why*. You measure all life and business decisions against the gold standard. As you continue making decisions that are consistent with your purpose, you will find that people listen to you. They actively seek out your opinions. Being authentic and honest with yourself and with others is not only easy; it is a way of life. There is a feeling of fulfillment. You can't wait to go to work because work is fun, it is your passion.

Seeing Why in action

Observing people and their enterprise actively pursuing their purpose and cause is branding at its finest. Soon others outside the organization will come to understand what the entity and those who work there stand for.

Cirque du Soleil is a good example. The Cirque describes itself as a "dramatic mix of circus arts and street entertainment." Unlike a traditional circus, Cirque performs a show that synthesizes circus styles from around the world, surrounded by a central theme and storyline.

Cirque's *Why* is to bring the same excitement to people they had when they were kids. To fulfill this purpose, every show is creative, innovative and entertaining. By design, they are colorful and fast moving. They design, produce and cast their shows by that standard. They create each show to fulfill their purpose of bringing the same excitement their audience had when they were kids.

Starbucks coffee is another example of seeing *Why* in action. Starbucks' purpose is to create a third place for people to go (home, work and Starbucks). That is why they have the comfy furniture and Wi-Fi. They have food, music and now cocktails.

Communicating internally and externally

All enterprise communications—either internal or external—must be consistent. They must reflect the enterprise's cause, its purpose and its *Why*.

This consistency of purpose appears in the company's statements of business strategy. It appears in the internal newsletter that reaches every employee. It is consistent and continuous communication. The company's values never change. Everyone lives them everyday.

External communications work the same way. The company's purpose and cause come across in its communications and customer relationship management. The audience for external communications includes not only customers but also vendors, investors, lenders and the public at large.

Remember Apple's *we think differently* statement? Apple's intent to disrupt the status quos of the computer industry appears everywhere. See it in how they answer the phone, in their advertising, in their PR image campaigns, in how they interact with customers. The message is, *we care about what's important to our customers*.

Whether communicating internally or externally, the enterprise's cause and purpose comes across in everything we say and do.

Chapter 2: Good Times or Bad, You're Still the CEO

No matter how your company or its industry is doing, regardless of either's prosperity, there are always challenges in being the CEO. People will forever look to you for guidance and to point the way. During good times, the press and the financial media will be searching for a story. The more dirt, the better. Should you and the enterprise you head step into their crosshairs, so much the better for them. During bad times, the public and the watchdog media is searching for an expose' and the perpetrator who caused it.

Use your Why as a moral compass

Being dead certain about your cause and purpose counts for a lot. For many who ponder the pros and cons of major decisions in life and in business, their *Why* serves as a guide and road map. Recall in Chapter 1 how Tony Hsieh of Zappos needed to take complete control over the company's customer experience. The drop shipments blocked a major part of that goal. Since Hsieh's purpose was to deliver happiness, his logic probably followed a course similar to this:

- Zappos exists to deliver happiness
- The only way to deliver happiness is to achieve total control over the quality of our customer's experience when they visit Zappos
- Drop shipments to third party enterprises block Zappos' control over a significant part of its customer's experience
- Eliminating drop shipments restores Zappos' total control over its customer experience.

Conclusion: Eliminate drop shipments. The short-term cost will be enormous. *Not* eliminating drop shipments impugns Zappos' mission and will eventually redirect the company's purpose to something we never intended.

Notice how this hypothetical line of reasoning keeps everyone's eye on the ball—the enterprise's cause and purpose. It is up to the CEO to maintain this focus. Without such strong guidance, the enterprise will surely lose its way at the very first opportunity.

This is not to say that the CEO never makes mid-course corrections. They are constantly making decisions that adjust the enterprise's track. They make these changes not because they've lost faith in their purpose, but because these course corrections keep the enterprise more closely tracking with the mission and purpose. The *Why* never changes; how you get there does.

What keeps the CEO up at night?

Every CEO I know faces a barrage of conflicting decisions. The best course of action always floats to the top of the heap. Those that do float to the top are no problem. The boss is left with just a couple of equally viable alternatives. From this select group of viable options, which to choose? This is the question that can keep the boss awake at night, especially when the margin of error is thin and the wrong choice can send the company into a tailspin.

Another category on the list of challenging decisions has to do with the company's cash balance. Some say the safest course is to hoard cash. That is what I have seen many nonprofit boards do. They figure they worked so hard raising this money that they want to keep it—regardless of the mission to serve their cause. As a result, their constituents suffer, the nonprofit deviates from its purpose, and their donors turn to other nonprofits more aligned with their own causes.

CEOs need to maintain a balance between having sufficient cash for operating purposes plus a safety net and making investments to grow the company and fulfill its purpose. For the boss, this often means knowing when to pull the trigger and plow that scarce cash back into the business.

How do you know when it's time? From my own experience as a CEO, I can tell you that one thing you *don't* do is test the water temperature by jumping into the deep end. When you try new ideas, be sure to validate them first. I am always asking, "*How would we test that?*" The best tests of decisions are large enough to yield a valid result, but small enough to avoid any damage should the decision being tested go wrong.

Once the decision test results are in, the proper choice begins to emerge; but as a thoughtful CEO, you're not done yet. The analysis and testing is only used as a reference point. The rest of the decision comes from pitting the top choice against the *Why*, the heart and the gut. A prudent boss asks, "*Does it feel right? Does it smell right? Is it in alignment with our cause and purpose?*" If the answer is still yes, then you just made up your mind.

Being the boss is a contact sport

The competition also keeps the boss up at night. How do you know when a competitor is about to make a move that will damage your company? Even worse, with technology growing and morphing into new areas, new competitors can come from places you never thought about before. A good example is the publishing industry and this very book. Digital media and the e-Books that are a major part have certainly stolen market share from the big print publishing houses. Indeed, the growth rate of e-Books is many times that of the hardcopy publishers. I imagine the CEO's of these hardcopy publishers are trying to figure out what to do.

The smart CEO's will see how they can capitalize on the technology that is so disrupting to their business model and make

A CEO's Secret Weapon

it their own. These are the CEOs who see their purpose as feeding information, education and entertainment to a market that is starving for good content. The others are fighting technological innovation. Take, for example, the music publishing industry; companies are suing their very own customers for copyright infringement if they copy a purchased CD onto a computer or digital player.

So what does the boss do? For starters, the best CEO's I know get out of their offices and on the road. They visit their customers and not just their biggest customers. They work to identify those customers that are strategically important to the company's cause and purpose—its *Why*. Contact with these customers is often a more informative conversation. Unlike the biggest customer, the CEO knows that losing such a small customer won't hurt the top or bottom lines, so they can just talk. The savviest CEOs understand that a group of similar small customers is often larger than that single large customer when combined. When the CEO figures out how the company's cause can improve life for this entire group, she will have truly done her job.

It's easy to get paranoid about a competitor you know little about. What do you do? Gather intelligence. The best CEOs get to know their competitors. They don't rely on intelligence gathered by the sales and marketing staff who normally attend the industry's trade shows. The CEO makes it a point to meet and spend some time with their counterpart at competing companies. Again, Tony Hsieh of Zappos is a good example of one CEO chatting up the competition.

Over the course of many years, Hsieh met with and got to know Jeff Bezos, the CEO of Amazon and one of Zappos' biggest competitors. As mentioned in Chapter 1, Hsieh used the company's cause and purpose as a business strategy; Zappos bet

A CEO's Secret Weapon

Ask, what would give advantage over competition

that by being good to its employees—paying for all health care premiums, spending on personal development and giving customer service reps more freedom than at any other call center—they would offer better service than the competition. The logic went, better service translates into repeat customers, which means lower marketing expenses, long-term profits and rapid growth. This strategy *seemed* to be working, but by 2005 it remained unproven. At the same time, Hsieh was getting to know Jeff Bezos. Amazon was interested in acquiring Zappos. However, Hsieh was worried that their culture and purpose would get lost in Amazon and eventually disappear. Acquisition talks broke off, but Hsieh and Bezos remained in contact.

Four years later, in 2009, Hsieh and Bezos met again. Since the two knew one another pretty well by then, the discussion revolved around the corporate cultures, goals, causes and the purposes of both enterprises. Surprisingly, both men realized their *Whys* were more alike than different. Amazon's acquisition of Zappos closed on November 1, 2009. Instead of an all cash deal as Amazon originally proposed, Hsieh had requested all stock. He felt that selling Zappos for stock rather than cash made it feel more like a marriage than a sell-out. By the first quarter of 2010, Zappos sales were up 50 percent—Hsieh's strategy of keeping one eye on the competition, getting to know them well and visiting their camp worked.

Life under a microscope

The CEO must have an even temperament. Of course, they celebrate the enterprise's victories. So too do they feel the bad times. However, there can be no extremes. As long as the cause and purpose continue on track, the CEO is happy. That's life under the microscope of public opinion. It's especially true for those who head publicly held companies as the financial media, analysts who follow the stock, investors, lenders, vendors and employees all watch the CEO. Whenever there's an issue, a display of emotion or a wrong word said in public, it hits the airwaves and everyone knows about it instantly. The stock price usually takes a dive.

For Henry Samueli, the co-founder of telecom giant, Broadcom, life under the microscope became a reality. Samueli created a very large company that, among other things, has one of its chips in most every cellular telephone. He is a family man and dedicated philanthropist. He created a company that hit the right market at the right time with the right technology. Broadcom soared.

Then, scandal hit. Samueli's cofounder and Broadcom's former chief executive officer, the flamboyant Henry Nicholas III, was indicted on fraud, conspiracy and drug charges, including allegations that he spiked the drinks of other executives with the drug, ecstasy. The indictment said he also maintained several residences used to distribute and sell drugs, including cocaine and methamphetamine, and that he threatened to kill people if they talked about his activities. The indictment said Nicholas and his guests had at one time inhaled so much marijuana on a flight to Las Vegas from Orange County, California, that clouds of smoke and fumes drifted into the cockpit of the private plane and the pilot had to put on an oxygen mask.

Adding to Samueli's nightmare at hearing this, Nicholas was also accused of hiring not only prostitutes for himself, for customers and associates of Broadcom, but to also have supplied them with drugs. As if that wasn't enough, Samueli himself was drawn into a string of accusations and indictments of backdating share option certificates. This incident cost the company $2.2 billion in stock write-downs. There is a somewhat bright spot for Samueli. He was later reinstated at Broadcom as Chief Technical Officer after a judge exonerated him of all charges.

The point of these stories is that if you want to be the boss, you had better prepare for life under the microscope. If your background cannot withstand such scrutiny, don't take the job.

Actual versus perceived responsibilities

For those who have never actually been the boss, there is usually a difference between perceived responsibilities and reality. Due to the media's relentless need to create and then sell a story, the public views CEOs as overpaid. They sit in a big office doing very little. Rather than doing any real work, they shuffle the dirty, tough and risky tasks to subordinates.

Reality is quite different. The boss can never stop working. When they are not sleeping, they are working. With modern technology, the boss is but an email or a text message away from the latest crisis. That's the way it should be. If the boss isn't actually at work, she is *thinking* about work.

The CEO can have no secrets—none, ever. If they head a public company, the salary and total compensation is wide open for public scrutiny. If they head a really big company, their personal health issues can literally move the market for the company's stock. Any breaks in their marital harmony become fodder for media sensation. Further, any problems with subordinates become your problem too as it is reflected back on your poor judgment at hiring such a dolt.

Amidst all these issues, to whom can the CEO turn to for advice? If it's a public company, very few and they have to be within the company. Providing confidential information to an outsider risks running afoul with the SEC's insider trading rules.

CEOs have a handful of things they must do. Though these are few in number, they carry enormous responsibility and encompass a wide area. The CEO's major responsibilities include:

- Guiding the enterprise along the course prescribed by the stated purpose and cause
- Executing the overall business strategy set forth by the board of directors
- Maintaining stewardship of company assets and deploying them in a manner that achieves the business plan

Even the boss reports to someone higher. The CEO reports to the board of directors. The board reports to stockholders and other investors. Ultimately, anyone on the board and the CEO are replaceable.

Maintain a culture of transparency and honesty in all company dealings especially when such public admissions will injure the company.

The difference between the founder and the CEO

During the formative years, often the founder is the CEO. How long this lasts is a function of the company's needs and the founder/CEO's capabilities. Nevertheless, there is a difference. Founders are the genius behind the company. They conceived the idea, developed a plan, created a business strategy and molded the enterprise around their own *Why*. Think of the founder as the true visionary and designer. It takes a special, unique talent to found a company, get it airborne and keep it aloft for any length of time.

The CEO, on the other hand, is the engineer who makes the founder's design and vision a reality. This too takes a special, unique talent. It is almost the difference between pure science (the founder) and applied science (the CEO).

A CEO's Secret Weapon

For a time during a start-up company's life, the founder may serve as CEO. Often this is as much a financial necessity as it is an executive need. However, successful companies usually outgrow the founder's capabilities. This is most often true of high technology companies. There, the founder is often an engineer. Eventually, the company will need the financial, sales, marketing, legal and management skills of a professional CEO.

What does an effective CEO look like?

Today, the boss must wear everyone's hat to a certain extent. Yes, they must hire specialists to head the various critical functions vital to the enterprise's operations. Nevertheless, they must still know a great deal about each of the disciplines for which their direct reports are responsible.

The most effective and successful CEOs are wonderful communicators. They speak with genuine conviction on their purpose and cause. The commitment and understanding of why they are here is contagious. The best CEOs possess the ability to be listened to and trusted by each of their constituent groups: employees, investors, other business leaders, vendors, customers, regulatory authorities and lenders. They carry a great deal of credibility.

Good bosses are flexible in their worldview as related to the company, its customers, its market, trends, technology innovations and legislation. Such flexibility is essential in a changing world. Where technology closes some doors, but opens new windows, the boss must respond. Where customers' needs change, the boss must have the means to respond ahead of time to capture greater market share or at least avoid losing what she has. Legislative changes can put a company out of business over night. This is especially true of today's financial services industry. The most effective CEO's anticipate changes and prepare for that contingency.

The boss must have one eye constantly on the horizon with the other watching their back. They must be not only their company's greatest advocate, but also its strongest, most honest critic. This must come through to the public. At the same time, they must be constantly questioning the assumptions on which the company's business model is based. The CEO knows that someday, somehow, these assumptions will deviate. When they do, the company must respond and adjust by adding or dropping products. They will use new technology and invest in new market segments.

CEOs who live their Why

There's a similarity among CEOs who live their *Why*. They live by a code of conduct. They have a compass that shows them the way even when others counsel them otherwise. Typically, such bosses find jobs for their people when they must let them go. However, it is not as effective as when the CEO jumps on the telephone and calls his counterpart at another company to tell her about the spectacular group of employees now available through no fault of their own and who are ready to work.

Cause and purpose oriented CEOs respect the public and customers. They understand and care about how the services they provide and products they produce affects those people.

Goldman Sachs is a bad example, but I suspect not atypical of the culture of greed surrounding Wall Street. Greg Smith, the former head of Goldie's US equity derivatives business in Europe and the Middle East, blew the whistle in a New York *Times* op-ed piece. There, Smith described the company as being without any sort of cause or purpose. He said that Goldman's culture, headed by CEO Lloyd Blankfein, has a single-minded focus on making money. To that end, the company routinely sacrifices the best interests of its clients (whom they call "muppets") to line their own pockets. Evidence of this is in so many of the municipalities that entered into interest rate swap contracts that have gone south. Many have paid hundreds of millions to unwind these ill-conceived contracts. Others are on the verge of bankruptcy. These are some of America's proudest towns: Harrisburg, PA; Stockton, CA; Vallejo, CA and Jefferson County, AL, to name just four. Smith claims the purpose of turning a profit by helping customers themselves make money was replaced by making money for the firm at the expense of the customers.

Working through the bad times

Rapidly growing companies have constantly changing requirements. These requirements exist in the equipment, in the real estate the company occupies, in its bank lines of credit and in its employees. At some point, the CEO realizes that some of the people who got them to where they are might not be the right ones to move them into the next phase of the business evolution. This is an awful decision to make.

Some people may still be useful and have a place at the company. However, they will no longer have a seat at the decision table. Others must be cashed out and wished well.

How does the CEO make such a decision and tell the people affected? At the end of the day, that is the CEO's job. That is why he earns his paycheck. The answer is, the boss delivers such bad news honestly, authentically and with total transparency. However it is done, it must be consistent with the CEO's and the company's cause and purpose—its *Why*.

Great leadership qualities in bad times

Leaders who guide their organizations through the rough patches all have a common style; they will never sugar coat the problems—after all, most problems are already obvious to everyone both inside and outside the enterprise. To do anything but tell the absolute truth would make them look like they didn't understand their own business and what was happening to it. Both offenses require removal from their post.

An example is Martha Stewart's insider trading problems, which at first had nothing to do with her company, Martha Stewart Omnimedia. Stewart sold $230,000 of ImClone Systems stock using information not yet available to the public. Given the amount of stock her co-defendants sold, Stewart was by far the smallest fish caught in the SEC's net. Her insider trading might have been survivable. Stewart's undoing was her lying about the stock sale, her conspiracy and her obstruction of justice. She served five months in prison, five months of home confinement, and two years of probation. Since convicted felons cannot be officers of publicly traded companies, Stewart was stripped of her offices at Omnimedia. Stewart's experience serves as a lesson: CEOs of companies going through difficult times must be completely transparent. Any indication that the image they portray is not transparent will raise questions of their ability to serve.

Another example is Juan Carlos I, the King of Spain as this book is written. It is up for debate how long he can hang onto the throne. King Juan had just called on his financially troubled country and its people to exercise frugality during Spain's extreme financial crisis with a record 23 percent unemployment. The 74 year-old monarch said all this as he was preparing to leave for a very expensive elephant-hunting safari in Botswana costing close to six figures (the cost for an elephant-shooting license alone is $26,000). King Juan Carlos is also the honorary president of the

Spanish branch of the World Wildlife Fund for Nature. Had King Juan not fallen and broken his hip while on safari, the public would have never discovered his extracurricular activities. Needless to say, the Spanish people were outraged over the lack of authenticity displayed by their King.

Bad times amplify the negative

Struggles bring out the worst in people. Companies are no different. During bad times, the CEO must adjudicate over turf wars between executives. People's survival instinct kicks in. Everyone is trying to become indispensible to ensure the ax doesn't fall on them.

During challenging situations, time accelerates and compresses. Decision-making time shrinks. This is no truer than with the company's finances. Bankers can smell trouble. When they do, they call in their loans like there's no tomorrow—because there just may not be. In our business climate of pre-packaged bankruptcies and assignments for the benefit of creditors, the CEO must act faster than ever to stave off a forced liquidation of his enterprise should it stumble. Where a CEO might have had six months to arrange alternative financing in the past, now they have just three months, if that.

Dealing with the Unexpected

Infamous for the battle of Little Big Horn, George A. Custer is believed to have said, *"It's not how many times you get knocked down but how many times you get up that counts."* This saying holds true for CEOs too. Unexpected events happen daily. They come from everywhere: Governmental regulators, competitors, vendors, customers, lenders, investors, new technologies that previously had nothing to do with the company. The list goes on.

Perceptive CEOs have a choice in how they manage the unexpected. Some will try fighting it and conquering the problem, others will investigate it as a potential opportunity.

Take a Houston furniture company for example. An arsonist set fire to the facility and burned it down. The owner and CEO was already a wealthy man. He could have just taken the insurance money, called it a career and retired, but he didn't do that. Long ago he identified his cause, his purpose and his *Why*. His belief in the American dream transferred to all his employees. He realized that they each had a choice where they wanted to work and he appreciated that they selected his company.

The employees appreciated the CEO right back. The company had a culture of setting goals, working hard and achieving those goals. This was a culture of success without compromise. It was built on 100 percent customer care and used mostly American-made products. These attributes composed the company's *Why*. Everything they did at this Houston furniture company aligned with this purpose and cause.

When the facility burned to the ground, there was no question in anyone's mind what to do. They rebuilt. Any other course of action would have opposed everyone's cause and purpose. The new facility was bigger, brighter and better than was its predecessor.

Was the arson that caused all of this expected? Certainly not. Was the fact that the company elected to rebuild expected? Absolutely. That is resilience with a capital "R".

Moneyball

As I compile this book the film, *Moneyball*, is in theaters. It's the story about the Oakland A's baseball team and their general manager, Billy Beane. As the story unfolds, it is obvious to me

A CEO's Secret Weapon

that Beane has a very clear vision of his cause. It is to change major league baseball forever. He wants to turn the reasons one team wins the World Series upside down.

Beane gets his chance. The A's owners are first businessmen whose mission is to make money. Oakland is at best a second tier market, probably a third tier. The fan base simply doesn't provide sufficient revenue to pay the player salaries of the first tier market teams like New York and Los Angeles. Beane finds his player salary budget, at just $41 million, the lowest in all of major league baseball—about 33 percent that of the New York Yankees who spent $125 million. Beane cannot afford top talent or even middle talent.

But Beane is resilient. He gets the chance to test his theory of why teams win. Using mathematical models and paradigms of predictive performance, he finds that player salaries have almost nothing to do with a team's ability to win. He assembles a team based on factors such as on-base percentage and slugging percentage rather than conventional batting average. Both attributes can be acquired for a fraction of the cost of players with .300 batting averages.

Turns out, Beane was mostly right. His Oakland A's—the lowest salaried team in professional baseball—cobbled together the longest winning streak in baseball history (19) and made it to the playoffs.

Billy Beane was similar to so many CEO's who have a tightly focused cause and purpose. He was uncompromising in his belief and pursuit of his cause. He refused to let the cost of a player's salary deter him. He found a way to beat the odds and accomplished it because he never lost sight of his *Why*.

Managing choices to maintain consistency of purpose

—Refuse to let others technology deter us change the conversation

35

Being the boss is a job of choices. As boss, you must select the best choices that are most likely to achieve your company's purpose. Let's use the fictional car manufacturer, Kaito, portrayed in the action-adventure novel, *Deadly Acceleration* by best-selling author, Chris Malburg. This story of industrial terrorism on a global scale is a good example of how one CEO maintains his consistency of purpose even as his cars begin crashing for no apparent reason.

At first a few hundred, then several thousand Kaitos suddenly accelerate out of control. The brake systems fail, transmission control stops. The cars become high-speed, runaway deathtraps. Then the onboard theft prevention system locks the steering wheel. Kaito drivers, their passengers and the victims their unguided missiles crash into are dying by the thousands.

Kaito Automotive's CEO, Noriko Kaito, remains steadfast in his purpose—to build the world's safest, most environmentally efficient cars. Throughout the book he sticks to his purpose even in the face of Congressional intervention and a command visit to the President's Oval Office. Kaito's competitors circle like vultures, doing everything possible to bring down the world's largest auto manufacturer. Not for a minute does Kaito's CEO lose faith in his company, that his engineers design the safest cars, or that his production people know how to build automobiles.

For any CEO, such a public display of the company's product failure is a nightmare. If such failure endangers and even kills innocent citizens, it becomes the worst-case scenario. That is certainly what Noriko Kaito is suffering in *Deadly Acceleration*.

Transparency means everybody knows

For publicly held companies, transparency in every aspect of the business is a fact of life. Anything less than complete candor can earn you a jail sentence. As the story earlier in this chapter of Martha Stewart demonstrated, the initial mistake is often survivable. But when combined with an ensuing cover-up, the public and the legal system have little capacity to forgive.

The media especially can sniff out any attempt at concealment. Suddenly, what began as just a humdrum business story becomes a *quest for the truth*. This is the stuff of which Pulitzer prizes are made. The reporter who first discovered it is no longer just doing her job. Instead, she is making a name for herself and possibly becoming world-famous. Her parents will be so proud.

CEO's must not only be truthful in fact, they must *appear* as truthful to a public that is skeptical and expert at ferreting out dishonesty. CEO's who are themselves authentic and live for their cause and purpose have a definite advantage. Their commitment comes through in everything they do and say.

How you react in public to the tough questions and what decisions you make involving the public also speaks volumes about your transparency. Let's take British Petroleum as a bad example once again. The company's continued legal maneuverings to wriggle out of paying the fines and cleaning up their safety violations in the face of the Deep Water Horizon disaster does not make them look any better. Indeed, such deliberate obfuscation of something that should be totally transparent continues to raise questions about the company's worthiness of the public's trust.

If you make a mistake

Everyone makes mistakes. As the CEO, you are responsible not only for your own mistakes, but for those of your employees, vendors, subcontractors and anyone else associated with the company. As this book is being written, Apple Computer is under the microscope for alleged abuses by one of its subcontractors, Foxconn, in China. Accusations are that Foxconn violated Apple's Supplier Code of Conduct by overcrowding in some of the housing provided to workers, employing complex pay structure overly relying on incentives, running an outdated payroll system and over-working employees and treating them harshly.

What do you do as CEO? First, take complete ownership of the problem yourself. Even though you probably had nothing to do with it, the company you head does. Next, apologize profusely and genuinely. Do it personally, facing those you harmed. Back up your apology with actions that are consistent with your cause, purpose and the *Why* of the organization as a whole.

If you do it right, the likely outcome is that people will believe you. They will forgive you. They will stand beside you. They will champion your cause and become your advocates. The impression such authenticity makes is that this CEO and those around her, are so committed to their beliefs that they are unwavering regardless of this awful situation.

When a *Why-centered* CEO faces a moral decision involving truth, honesty and transparency, there really is no decision at all. The CEO will always go the way of the *Why*. There is no choice. The *Why* is who he is. He would no sooner go against that moral imperative than do something terribly wrong.

Next in Chapter 3 you learn how to weather the storm of public criticism.

* * *

Chapter 3: Iceberg, Dead Ahead!

You can't do the same thing harder to get better results. Sometimes you just have to do things differently.

Being the CEO is like sailing a ship through arctic waters—it's 90 percent sheer boredom and 10 percent utter terror. Many mid-level executives could navigate the corporate ship through calm waters. Such an autopilot cruise is not really what the CEO is paid for. Shareholders and investors want someone they can count on when finding their way through an ice field. Make no mistake; there will be icebergs, hurricanes and all manner of storms. When adversity strikes, everything seems to go wrong at the worst time. You need a good person in a storm.

Arthur Golden described adversity in *Memoirs of a Geisha* as, "...a strong wind...it holds us back from places we might otherwise go. It also tears away from us all but the things that cannot be torn, so that afterward we see ourselves as we really are, and not merely as we might like to be."

The point is that the CEO must be totally grounded in reality—certain of his purpose and cause, his *Why*—to sail the enterprise out of stormy waters. When crisis hits, the hurricane-force winds of public scrutiny will strip away and lay bare for all to see every half-truth and outright lie. CEOs are left with only their cause and purpose to guide them. Throughout this chapter, we will identify the attributes necessary for a CEO to lead during the harshest of times.

Resilience is the key to survival

It's not the crisis, but how we *respond* to the crisis that defines us. CEOs have a different perception of how they define crises. A mid-level parts manager at an automotive manufacturing plant might define a crisis as the looming bankruptcy of a major supplier of dashboard components. The CEO, on the other hand, might look at the same fact set and see an opportunity. Finally now is the opportunity to take in house a critical component pipeline. She could buy the dashboard supplier and their assets *and* provide a financially stable place to work for its employees. By going vertical, the CEO sees an opportunity to increase gross margins where none existed before. That's resilient thinking.

Taking inventory of your resilience

The best way to avoid the icebergs through which you are guiding your corporate ship is to identify your resilience shortcomings and fix them before they become a problem. The most easily identified components of resilience include:

- Impulse control
- Optimism
- Self-efficacy
- Knowing when to seek help

Impulse control

CEOs seldom have the luxury of displaying an ill-considered impulse. They are constantly in the public eye—if not the media's, then the employees', the board's, customers', investors' or lenders'. A poorly timed outburst or a misunderstood reaction can unravel a reputation in an instant.

Part of being resilient is to control public displays of your first reaction to a question or an event. For example, wait for a few beats before answering what might at first appear as a reporter's antagonistic question intended to ambush you into a newsworthy outburst. To the audience, your pause appears merely as the time taken to consider your answer—certainly acceptable, in fact, creditable. In those brief seconds, think about the meaning behind the question—what is the interrogator's real purpose? Why would they ask such a question? What are they trying to get you to say or do? How does your answer fit into your cause, purpose and your *Why*?

Now that you've grabbed control over your first impulse to berate the reporter for asking such a blatantly destructive question, you can craft your answer around the conclusions you formed during your brief pause. Many adept CEOs take the opportunity to get the audience on their side. They do this with a preamble. Here's an example:

George, I can well understand why you ask. People want—and deserve—an answer. Transparency in everything this company does is important to us all—from the board of directors to our hardworking employees, valued customers and the community we serve. The truth is...

Then, for God sake tell the absolute truth. Part of impulse control is shutting your mouth before a lie can escape. If seeking the truth is a component of your cause and purpose, then this should be no problem. If the truth doesn't paint such a pretty picture, do not try to spin it or embellish it to lessen the damage. The error of omission is just as bad. Such cover-ups are obvious anyway. They only beg the question, *what else aren't you telling us?* It casts a pall of incredulity over everything else you say.

However, often there are times when the CEO cannot disclose certain truths. Perhaps the company is involved in an on-going lawsuit. Maybe it is involved in constructing spy satellites and cannot discuss the nature of its latest contract with the National Reconnaissance Office. There are a number of credible reasons you may be unable to disclose the entire situation. If you find yourself in this predicament, then say so. Here's how to do it politely:

George, I would like to answer your question. However, it is public knowledge that the company is in its quiet period leading up to the stock offering set for June 25th. SEC rules prohibit me from disclosing anything about our financial prospects to you or anyone. If I were to answer your question, our stock offering would be shelved, our current shareholders and new investors would suffer and I could face prosecution. You wouldn't want me jailed for answering your question, now would you? I didn't think so. Just as soon as the SEC-mandated quiet period is over, I will answer all of your questions.

Such an honest answer does a number of things, including creating a high level of credibility for you. It also puts a stop to such questions and gives an honest, real reason why. Honest answers almost always make you look good, even when the news isn't the best.

How often have you heard that we are what we think? The most important work that we do is keeping our thoughts under control. The same habit goes for home and family as well as work. I'm not suggesting that anyone become an unemotional robot. However, there's a big difference between the person who makes it a habit of spewing forth a stream-of-consciousness diatribe and the person who takes a moment to organize her thoughts.

Once organized, present your case in a way that makes sense. Begin by first constructing the case on theory. Then support that theory with proven facts. Once the facts are out, close with the logical conclusion—the only conclusion anyone could have in the face of such a well-presented case. Then stop. Continuing to sell your position after you've made your case simply raises the question how much you really believe what you just said. Over time, people will appreciate the short, concise and logical way you think and speak. Your credibility will grow.

Optimism

A CEO's Secret Weapon

Would you sail on a ship whose captain you heard expressing worry that the ship was going to sink? Would you board an airplane whose captain announced over the main cabin intercom that the plane was likely to crash? Certainly not.

Every leader needs a heavy dose of optimism—especially when there's trouble. It encourages people to rise to the occasion and become better than they thought they were. However, it must be *credible* optimism based on fact, as people will immediately see through happy words that have no basis and the person voicing them will soon lose all credibility. Their ability to lead will evaporate like water thrown on a hot griddle.

When trouble looms, gather your team around you. It is their counsel and advice that helps the CEO form a credible plan of attack. The more input the team provides to the crisis, the more ownership they feel. They will not let something of their own creation fail.

Where your team lacks the technical knowledge required, go and get it. If that knowledge can be found within the company, so much the better. If you need to go outside, then hire the best, most knowledgeable and experienced people you can and temporarily attach them to your team.

Create a culture of controlled urgency with well thought out steps. Have a single spokesperson—preferably the CEO. People want to see the captain and hear the conviction in her voice that all will soon be well.

Some CEOs should not be at the helm under any circumstances during a crisis. These bosses haven't internalized the organization's cause and purpose. Their *Why* is different from the others'. Often such individuals are merely hired hands with an apparently good-looking resume.

Take, for example, Lehman Brothers' former CEO, Richard Fuld. Under his dubious leadership, Lehman Brothers declared an excess of liabilities over assets and went bankrupt. The shuttering of one of the largest banks in the securities world put thousands of employees out of work and cost them hundreds of millions in lost retirement funds. The federal bankruptcy court appointed Anton Valukas, a prominent Chicago lawyer and former United States attorney, to conduct an investigation to determine what happened over at Lehman. Valukas' 2,200-page report found that there was enough evidence for a prosecutor to bring a case against top Lehman officials—Fuld included—and its auditor, Ernst & Young, for misleading government regulators and investors.

Contrast that independent revelation with Lehman's mission statement that Fuld was responsible for executing and upholding:

"We are one Firm ... defined by our unwavering commitment to our clients, our shareholders, and each other. Our mission is to build unwavering partnerships with and value for our clients, through the knowledge, creativity, and dedication of our people, leading to superior returns for our shareholders."

Who knows what Dick Fuld was thinking during Lehman's final days? It could be that in trying to fool the regulators, clients and his own employees about the bank's precarious capital shortage, he ended up fooling himself. Therein lies the real danger for any CEO.

Self-efficacy

This is a term used in psychology, dealing with someone's belief in their own competence. Every CEO has a significant belief in their own abilities to perform in a specified manner to attain pre-defined goals. If they didn't, then they would not last very long at the helm. Belief in your own capabilities affects your social interactions in almost every way.

Self-efficacy goes hand-in-hand with people's perception of you. Their perception must tie directly with your own self-perception. Anything different means that you probably don't realize the impression you are making on people. This makes for a highly inefficient form of communication.

Take for example, the tough-as-nails CEO who runs over his subordinates, leaving behind road kill. "I don't run a kindergarten here," he says. "If I'm tough, it's because I believe in them and know they can do better. Everyone knows that." No, they don't. Such an attitude may work for some hierarchical organizations like the Army or a police department. However, in a commercial enterprise it stifles creativity and people's opinions. The boss is left with the entire organization resting on his shoulders. People are simply doing exactly what he says to do and they share no responsibility for results because the boss refused to listen to them.

Bring who you really are to the table all the time. If you believe in your people, don't hide behind a concrete wall of tough authority that never allows for constructive dissent.

Seek help when needed

It takes a CEO who is secure in her position within the company to seek help when it's needed. The easiest help is technical in nature. No one expects the CEO to have the requisite technical knowledge in a field in which she has no background. However, what about capabilities in an area closer to the CEO's own skill set? Say, executive team building. Some would say the board hired the CEO to build a world-class team. Why the need for an expert?

How do you suppose the board got that idea? It might have come from the CEO herself. Some people think they must present the image of someone who is an expert in all things. Even though it's absurd, there are those who will hold such people to the standards they created themselves, just to see them fail.

The way around such pitfalls is to stick to your cause and purpose. There is no better expert than the CEO who conceived of the cause, built an organization to pursue it and is steadfastly committed to its success. Bringing experts and outside help in to further the cause only affirms that commitment. When I see such a CEO, I see someone who is relentlessly pursuing their belief and will do whatever it takes to succeed. That's the person you want on the bridge steering the ship.

When perception is not reality

Be intentional about the perceptions people have of you. If they aren't accurate, or if the signals you are sending do not portray you as you really are, change them. Your own self-perception should integrate closely with your cause and purpose—the *Why*. If the messages you send out are authentic and honest, people will perceive you as one with your cause.

The *How* introduced in Chapter 1 is closely aligned with this concept. If the *Why* is your cause, then the *How* is the set of guiding principals that enable you to achieve your purpose and cause. Often people mention the traits of trust, honesty and integrity when describing just how they achieve their purpose. Here's how:

Trust: The CEO trusts in people's ability to identify with and commit to the purpose to which he has as well.

Honesty: If the CEO exhibits dead-on honesty about who he is and what his purpose is, then people will fairly judge. Either they believe the CEO is capable of reaching the stated goal and they sign on to join him, or they don't. In that case, they will leave.

This happens often when you see two executives competing for the top spot. There can only be one CEO. The one not chosen often leaves the company. They decide that their cause and purpose was really to run the show. They never really believed in the organization's *Why*. It's a similar situation to Sam Langley when he was competing against the Wright Brothers to be first to fly. When he didn't reach that goal, he quit rather than try building on the Wright's achievement and furthering the cause of manned flight.

Integrity: This goes to the consistency of purpose. The CEO's actions must be consistent with the cause. They cannot say one thing (the *Why*) but act in a contrary way. Richard Fuld of Lehman Brothers seemed to do that as his company was crumbling. Rather than let the customers and investors know the firm was insolvent and that they should not risk their own capital by dealing with Lehman (as their mission statement said they probably should), he lied. He tried to get huge loans to bolster Lehman's capital position; he tried to convince the firm's counterparties to a number of risky transactions that Lehman had sufficient capital to make good on their contractual commitments when it did not and Fuld knew it did not.

The CEO's 360 degree review

How do you know how people really see you? There is a way, but it isn't comfortable for some CEO's and it takes some courage to participate. The CEO's 360-degree review is exactly what it says—the CEO is reviewed from *all* sides. Board members participate, peers do, subordinates do, customers are invited to participate, so are vendors and sometimes lenders and investors. Anyone with regular contact is a candidate for participating in the CEO's 360.

There is usually a structure to the 360. Often this takes the form of a set of questions to answer about the CEO and the interaction she has with the person. The goal is to get the person's impression of the CEO's performance, image, capabilities and management style among a number of other index points. The CEO gets to see all the answers and often initiates a dialog with some of the responders. There is no argument nor is there any chance for retribution. The board, which oversees the 360, makes sure of that. They want everyone's honest participation. Those CEOs who survive, come out better people for the experience. The results are sometimes surprising. Especially for those CEO's without a clue about the impression they make on others. Here's an example:

Confused customer service

A case of confused intent surfaced when a company asked a major customer to participate in a CEO 360. That customer's impression of the CEO was of someone who had failed to build any bench strength among his staff. The CEO was shocked.

"I am absolutely focused on customer service. That is what I am about," he said.

The customer answered, "Then why do you send me emails at 2 a.m. leaving unnecessarily detailed answers to questions I never raised? If you are working until 2 a.m. so often, then you have problems more serious than customer service at your company. And the detail of your answers—why do you even know about such things? I certainly don't, nor do I care. That's what I pay my mid-level managers for. If I were to take the time diving into such minutiae, I'd be doing the job of someone else rather than doing my job. I have plenty of my own work and don't need to find more elsewhere."

Get 360 from Michael

The CEO's takeaway was that customer service actually meant hiring smart, responsible people who were committed to treating customers consistent with the company's purpose and cause, then empower them with all the authority they required to do their job.

The CEO creates an expensive bottleneck

A CEO at an electronics distributor discovered that he actually created problems rather than solving them—expensive problems at that. This particular CEO (of a company whose annual revenue exceeded $1 billion) insisted on reviewing every invoice before it went out to the customers. The treasurer, who participated in this CEO's 360, brought up the point that he had to increase the company's working capital line of credit by an additional $80 million because the CEO typically had 27 days of invoices on his desk just sitting there awaiting review. The stack of invoices was a foot high and represented real money that wasn't being paid to the company because the CEO couldn't seem to get around to reviewing them. Because of the CEO's 360, the treasurer installed a set of efficient internal controls that ensured invoice accuracy and bypassed the CEO's unnecessary review entirely. The company saved $3.2 million a year in interest expense on money they no longer had to borrow.

Think before you write

A final example of a 360 revelation came when a participating customer suggested that the CEO might have a substance abuse problem. The board was shocked since everyone knew the CEO never drank anything stronger than a Diet Coke or take more than an Advil. The CEO went to the customer and asked how she had made such a wrong impression. "Well," said the customer it's your late night emails. They just aren't as coherent as those I get from you during the day. I just assumed you were in your cups by then."

It turned out the CEO was sleep deprived—a problem she created herself. By 11 pm, she was so tired that those emails she sent were ripe with misspellings, grammar mistakes and disjointed logic. The take-away is that you need to assess your physical and mental condition before interacting with people. If you aren't capable, have a temporarily diminished capacity, or for whatever reason are not up to the task, don't risk your credibility by trying to be a hero.

Sharing the truth—do I have to?

By not giving people the full picture, you put yourself and your company at the mercy of their active imaginations. People will fill in the blanks—usually with their worst fears or with whatever fills their personal agenda—half-truths, lies and damn lies. The media is famous for this—sleaze and dirt sell. The more a reporter can draw into question someone's actions or, better yet, those of an entire enterprise, the better chance the pitch to their editor will be green-lighted. At that point, the slant of the story is locked, regardless of the truth that their reporting may reveal. Here is how such a conversation might sound:

"Dr. Barr," says the reporter from a financial markets television show, *"I would like you to comment on allegations that Company X has used accounting window dressing to cover up the fact that they have insufficient capital to make their next $250 million bond interest payment."*

"I've heard those allegations. They are not factual," I say. *"The fact is that the company just reported its quarterly balance sheet and shows its debt interest coverage stands at 2.1 times. Those numbers were reviewed by its public accounting firm and signed off by the CEO and CFO."*

"I'm sorry, Dr. Barr, but that's not the direction my editor wants this story to go. I will have to seek other sources that can support my premise."

Admittedly, this fictional conversation is a bit out of the mainstream. Most reporters are at least a little more ethical. However, the point is that sometimes, no matter what the truth is, people will not let it get in the way of the direction in which they are headed.

The impact of being honest

Some fear the fallout of revealing an ugly truth about themselves, their employees or the enterprise they lead. Certainly, the impact—at least in the short term—may well be negative. Investors may run for the hills. Company stock may tank. However, the reason you are there and doing what you do is a much longer-term proposition. The near-term fallout may sting, but it doesn't change your ultimate cause, your *Why*.

Recall the earlier example of Martha Stewart. Had she simply admitted a temporary lapse in judgment when she authorized trading her ImClone stock based on inside information, she probably wouldn't have gone to prison. She might even have turned state's evidence and actually come out the hero. Stewart might have even hung onto her corporate positions at Omnimedia. But no, Martha Stewart chose to lie about her involvement in the scheme. She traded short-term convenience for what turned out to be a felony conviction that will dog her for the rest of her gilt-edged life.

The impact of being honest will ultimately help your credibility with those who count. People understand how difficult it must be to suck it up and admit that something horrible happened, offer a solution, make recompense and move on. Such a selfless act speaks volumes about an individual's integrity. When the next crossroads comes (and it certainly will), the person's past refusal to take the easy way out enhances their current credibility. People reason that if they told the truth about such an awful past event, then they must be telling the truth about the latest, not-so-awful event. Such an individual becomes the go-to person not only for the truth, but also to lead the organization out of the mess in which it finds itself.

Making the truth more palatable

Spinning the truth to your own advantage is seldom—if ever—a good idea. First, people are smart. They can see right through such trickery. When they do, two things happen:
- The spin-meister loses credibility
- People smell a cover-up

Then suddenly what might have began as a minor incident, hardly worth mentioning, becomes the *cause de jure*. You become the story rather than the once minor incident. Never, ever leave people with the impression that you think you are smarter than them. You are not. Usually, these are the very people who hired you and can fire you.

Never minimize the seriousness of an issue or incident. If you're going to make a mistake, err on the side of overstating the problem. It speaks of your concern and how seriously you take the problem. If you've overstated it, then people will come to their own conclusions and be more willing to forgive. Spinning the truth to make it seem less than it is, does not further your cause or purpose. If you are looking for *Why*, you won't find it in spinning.

Behind closed doors

If you subscribe to the ideal of total transparency, then there are no closed doors. What you and your people discuss in private are the same things that you would not cringe at seeing in the headlines of the newspaper. If your cause is worthwhile and the ways in which you pursue it are equally commendable, you actually *want* people to see the inner workings of your operation.

At this writing, President Obama is being called out on the carpet for saying something in confidence to Russian President Dmitry Medvedev. Unbeknownst to Obama, an open mike caught and recorded him telling Mr. Medvedev—thereby telling his patron, the once-and-future Russian President Vladimir Putin—that he will have 'flexibility' on Russian demands opposing a U.S. missile defense for Europe after the American election.

President Obama was caught saying in effect that he is ready to do something the Russians will like but that the American people won't. This severely diminished the American President's credibility among his constituency. The question became one of:

Are you really working for the cause of the American people or are you just trying to get yourself reelected?

Maintaining such a closed-door policy forces the boss to say, *I know better than you do and you should just trust me.* Calling for that thumbs up or down decision is something no leader ever needs to force on their constituency. The answer may well come back that you haven't earned their trust or that you have succeeded in losing it. Either way, they may be unwilling to bet their next paycheck on your ability to lead.

Speak to be remembered

A good CEO not only wants people to remember what she says, but also to *repeat* it to others. This is a premeditated, conscious effect. There is nothing wrong with orchestrating the likely outcome of your presentation whether you are speaking to thousands or just heading a meeting of five people. Plan for what you get and get that for which you plan. How do you do that?

First, figure out what you want from the presentation, the goal. Determine precisely the ending perception or action you want from your audience. From there, figure out the best way to achieve that reaction.

With the end firmly defined, all that remains is filling in the mechancs of the presentation. Almost. The speakers who are best remembered are those who appear to be talking *with* their audience rather than *to* them. A CEO who is a good communicator can appear to wing it. They can do this because they know their subject and their audience inside and out.

Be aware of your body language. Sitting around the boardroom table slouched and fidgety sends one message. Good posture, sitting up straight and following the conversation sends quite another message—that you are engaged in the proceedings and an active participant.

It's true that clothes don't make the man or the woman. However, the *right* clothes send a message too. For example, an open jacket says that you are relaxed and have nothing to hide. No jacket with shirtsleeves rolled up says that you are among peers and friends and want to hear their ideas.

If you disagree with others in a meeting, ease into your differences politely and considerately. It never hurts to acknowledge the merits of the opposition's argument and the effort they went through in constructing it. Using a phrase such as, "*You might wish to consider…*" opens the door for your ideas without shutting out your audience.

If you need everyone to agree on a particular outcome from a meeting, line up a champion or two you know will help you ahead of time. Also, people's affinity and commitment should be to the enterprise's cause and purpose rather than to any individual's.

The *Why* is stronger than any single individual. They will break their back to avoid letting down the group.

Hewlett-Packard under Carli Fiorina was famous for having a special meeting of key department heads called, *morning scrum*. You've likely seen scrums before at rugby matches. The players stand in a circle, arms around each other's shoulders, heads bent toward the middle. Fiorina's morning scrum didn't usually last very long. The executives voiced problems, concerns and coordinated with one another for the day's goals. At that point, they were a team. They behaved as a team and communicated as team members.

The art of subtle persuasion

To be clear, persuading is not the same as coercing. We're talking about getting someone to see your point and agreeing with you. Persuasion is simply taking someone to a place they would have gotten to eventually by themselves anyway. Coercing, on the other hand, forces someone to do something that is against their free will. It is a negative thing. Persuasion is not.

The most effective CEO's are persuasive in a subtle manner. They recognize the fact that most people just want to please. The CEO simply gives them that opportunity. For example, if you find yourself explaining the organization's cause and purpose—the *Why*—be sure to allow your audience to evaluate it for themselves. Don't ever try to close a sale before the buyer reaches their own conclusions about the deal. Until that time, you still have some explaining to do.

Show, don't tell

People like to be *shown* rather than be told. Sometimes, the most persuasive arguments come by way of a story rather than a set of principals handed down to the masses from on high. Stories that persuade have three parts: A beginning, middle and an end.

55

The beginning shows a conflict that needs resolution, the middle shows how the conflict is resolved and the end shows the results attained and the moral to the story. Character development adds more interest as people will know a little something about who this person is and how she got herself into this situation. Ratcheting up the stakes if she fails adds even more interest once you get your audience to care just a little bit about your character.

You don't have to be a bestselling novelist to craft a story for use as a persuasive example. Nor does it have to be true. In fact, limiting yourself to a true story makes it unnecessarily difficult to create the story. Simply begin by; *What if there was a guy...* It's that simple.

The best communicators listen to their audience's questions and guide the conversation more than they talk. They allow the audience to form their own conclusions. It just so happens those conclusions usually parallel those of the CEO/speaker. It often happens that people realize they were always in agreement with the speaker's arguments—she just explained them better is all.

Recall the Houston furniture company I talked about earlier. Yes, an arsonist burned their facility to the ground. Certainly, they rebuilt because the CEO had inspired his own purpose and cause in his employees. They all shared the same *Why*. How did he do that?

His *Why* was the American dream—anyone can do anything here in this country if they are willing to work hard and never lose sight of their goal. It is compelling on several levels. First, it is a worthwhile cause. It is also simple and easily repeated in a consistent manner to avoid confusion. Finally, it is compelling. Who wouldn't want to achieve their goals simply by working hard?

A CEO's Secret Weapon

But this particular CEO did something that went without saying—literally. He *acted* out his purpose. He proved his cause by seeking out workers from the worst parts of Houston. He trained them and gave them a chance to live the American dream. He worked by their side in the trenches. He would never ask them to do something that he wouldn't do himself. They often saw him doing just that. He led by his good example and often didn't have to say a word.

This Houston furniture company owner was loved and respected by his employees. They wanted to please him and emulate him. He gave them every chance to do just that. Soon the employees spoke of his cause and purpose as if it were their own—because it was. What once was just one man's *Why* now had many, many sponsors who were equally committed. If there was ever a subtle persuasion, it flourished big time in this Houston furniture company.

Many people practice the art of persuasion with the high-stakes meetings over which they preside. It seems the more there is as stake, the more prep time the presentation warrants. That's true. However, what's wrong with taking that same attention to detail and using it on *all* your presentations, regardless of what is at stake? Soon such attention to detail and the favorable outcomes it elicits becomes a habit. Eventually, your meetings and presentations become so much more productive because they achieve what you want.

Chapter 4 shows how to identify what is really important in those high-stakes conversations we all have.

* * *

Chapter 4: High Stakes Conversations: Talking About What Matters

If you are the CEO, almost every conversation you have with anyone in your company or outside it is a high stakes conversation. It becomes so important because of who you are, the power you wield, and the office you hold. Choose your words carefully. Believe in the law of unintended consequences. Anything you say can and will be used against you should things go awry.

Before you open your mouth to speak, imagine that you are the largest cog in the center of interconnected gears. Your gear rotates just a few teeth clockwise. The gear linked to you is slightly smaller—perhaps it belongs to one of your senior VPs. That gear moves an entire half turn. The gear next to the SVP is smaller still. It rotates two turns to the SVP's half turn. And down the line, it goes. The result is an awful lot of gears spinning wildly throughout the organization because you made one small move. Perhaps you were just testing an idea. Maybe you didn't even mean what you said.

The point is, that high stakes conversations can occur when you least expect them and can have unintended consequences if you're not careful. Throughout this chapter, we'll identify the difference between real conflict and dissention and how to use both. You'll see how the pros prepare for high-stakes conversations—the results really are premeditated. Choosing the right venue for your meeting can mean the difference between success and something less. Chapter 4 closes with some ideas on just how you can shape people's perceptions.

Managing Conflict

A CEO's Secret Weapon

Conflict is a fact of business life. Mastering conflict and controlling it is essential. Conflict blocks any true conversation about what really matters. It gets mired in emotions, defensive moves, and all sorts of other irrelevancies to the issue at hand. This is not to say the CEO should ignore conflict. You can't. Nevertheless, before you can move any highstakes conversation forward, you must first resolve the conflicts blocking the way.

Emotion—someone's hurt feelings or perception of a threat—usually dwells at the heart of most business conflicts. Someone has to be the adult in the conversation. That task ultimately falls on the CEO's shoulders. To uncover the emotion and remove it from an otherwise meaningful conversation, follow these steps:

Step 1: Stick to the facts

Conflicts are ripe with misunderstandings and errors in fact. Uncover and expose them for all to see. Some are honest errors. Others were planted deliberately to derail the agenda; think of these as land mines. Once exposed, it is your responsibility as the leader to disarm them so they cannot be used again, and turn the group in the right direction.

Step 2: Distill the issue

State the conflict—now devoid of errors—in just a few very simple sentences. This statement must omit all emotion. Now you're ready to resolve the conflict. It is usually between two parties—perhaps the leaders of entire departments. Whoever the actors are, force them to resolve the conflict so you can move on, furthering the organization's cause, purpose and *Why*.

Step 3: What if you can't resolve the conflict?

Failure is not an option. If Steps 1 and 2 fail to produce results, reorient the resolving conversation to one of curiosity—your curiosity. This new tact will dominate those who might still be angry. Curiosity plays on people's desire to be reasonable.

Even though you might be a senior executive or the CEO, for now become a *learner*. Find out why the principals involved in the conflict feel the way they do. You are no longer the judge and jury—you are now the mediator. You are curious about their feelings. People love to talk about how they feel. It purges their emotions. If you let them talk long enough, their anger will evaporate.

If time is short—as it always seems to be—and you can't wait for the verbal venting to stop, here's a shortcut. Get the person who needs to vent to write down (yes, old school using paper and pencil) everything that happened. Make them use painstaking detail. However—and here's the catch—no one will ever see their written venting. It is for their eyes only. What works is the *process* of doing it. The physical act of handwriting on paper their real and imagined slights is cathartic and very therapeutic. Soon they will have exhausted themselves and be ready to reenter the adult world.

Harnessing dissention

Dissention has a bad rap. There's nothing wrong with dissention. I have yet to meet a truly effective CEO who surrounds herself with sycophants. You don't have all the answers—no CEO does. Moreover, not every idea coming out of your mouth is golden. Amazing, but true nevertheless. Encourage constructive dissention. Embrace it as the creative mill it is. Encourage your people to disagree and pick apart an idea or a business strategy. If it can't stand up to this scrutiny, then it wasn't really the golden idea you had originally thought. You just saved the cause a whole lot of time and money by not planting a tree that would ultimately bear no fruit.

Dissention often has a habit of sliding into conflict. People want to be heard and their ideas, accepted. To prevent constructive dissention from slipping into the morass of conflict, deflect it in another direction. Simply remind the combatants of the true purpose of the meeting, and how it will further the ultimate cause and reason everyone is working here. Then ask, "Are you still on board with that?" This simple question has a monumental effect. It goes to the very heart of the person's belief system and why they joined the organization in the first place.

Some CEOs are afraid of dissention. They mistake dissention for conflict. They take disagreement personally. Get over it. Running an enterprise is not a democracy; however, it cannot appear as a dictatorship either. One thing is sure, it's definitely not easy. If it were, anyone could do it and the investors wouldn't need you. The key to successful dissention is to control it so that everyone gets a say, new ideas are evaluated fully, and no one is ever penalized for disagreeing with the CEO.

One last point about dissention and conflict: never, ever avoid either. When a meeting or event is sure to have a fair amount of dissention and conflict, some CEO's send a surrogate in their place. They claim not to have the time for such petty issues. Nonsense. That's what the CEO does. By not getting down in the trenches with your people, you send the message loud and clear that they don't matter to you as human beings. The most important part of your personal success and that of your cause, accelerates the achievements of those who work for you. Ignoring them, their ideas and their feelings puts your mission in jeopardy.

Aggressive vs. Assertive

Male CEOs generally have little trouble making their demands known. If they are assertive and perhaps sometimes a little aggressive, they're just being the boss. Such behavior doesn't label them as anything but a gung-ho, can-do manager who gets the job done. High-stakes conversations and talking about what really matters rarely suffer from such a reputation. Indeed, I don't see anything wrong with it.

However, if you are a female CEO, you have something of a challenge ahead of you. The glass ceiling that once kept women out of the executive suite is shattering. Some industries are more progressive than others. Still, there's a double standard for interpreting the different ways men women communicate.

Diplomatic assertiveness

Being an effective leader and a woman at the same time requires a deft touch. Don't say, "You don't care if they call you a bitch, just as long as you get the job done." That style of browbeating leadership won't be successful for long. Eventually, you will no longer be considered a team player and the team will ease you out.

Just know that there will always be people who find fault with authority. When facing someone with strength and resolve to succeed, these same people become intimidated—especially when it's a woman exhibiting such strength. Some people avoid accountability by attacking others. If you're going to war with such people, make it a war that you can win.

The winning strategy is one of *diplomatic assertiveness*. Using a tempered, considered touch when you'd really rather stick your face right in his will more likely get what you want over the long haul. CEOs who are diplomatically assertive don't back down. Instead, they practice the art of presenting their ideas in ways that others can understand and support.

Allowing your adversaries to agree with you while saving face at the same time is an essential skill. Diplomatic assertiveness means pursuing agreement to a conclusion rather than continued argument without solution. Here are three tips for CEOs of both genders to use when practicing diplomatic assertiveness:

Tip #1: Build a team of loyal followers

Allow people to disagree with you. Listen to their arguments. Concentrate on winning the whole war, not just one little skirmish. Even though you probably have the one point that will nullify their argument, keep your powder dry. Instead, focus on building the agreement and loyalty necessary to implement the changes really needed.

Listen for any worries that your strategy creates among the staff. When someone has an idea, concentrate on their unvoiced doubts. Draw these doubts from them and put them on the table. This is how an idea is given a full and complete examination. Without it, they will go away thinking that you railroaded them. When you name their worries and acknowledge their beliefs, people feel a part of the whole. They hear your answer to their concerns and are more willing to listen to your alternative viewpoint.

As leader, you need to hear disagreement to make smarter decisions as a result. Demanding your way and refusing to listen to anyone else's ideas just keeps you in the dark; whereas giving everyone their say, even if you end up using your idea, builds loyal support. Who knows, you just may hear an idea that's better than yours. Hard to believe, but it could happen.

Tip #2: Jump the chasm

Let's say you have sat patiently by while a team member outlines her strategy. You don't interrupt and you sit up straight and pay attention. Such body language says that you are interested in hearing what she has to say. Still, you know that your ideas will work far better. Now what? Find the common ground. Let them save face.

Here's how. Say, *"I understand why you think A, B and C. Frankly, I'm glad you brought it up. I'm worried about them too. I can see our goals are aligned perfectly. You've opened my eyes to something different here. Even though my strategy is a little different from yours, we both finish in the same place. My solution takes a different direction than yours because of my experience in ..."*

Tip #3: Lead a revolution, not a rebellion

Rebellions start and end with complaints and blame. Few decisions ever come out of rebellion—their mission is to overthrow. The organizers appear self-righteous and usually self-serving if the rebellion is designed to put them in control.

Revolution, on the other hand, inspires people to join in creating something new and better for the overall good. Revolution builds on the possibilities of hope. One thing to remember: Revolutions take longer than rebellions and coups. Take care about announcing start and finish dates for your revolution. If you don't achieve them, people tend to lose faith.

Preparing the field of battle

Some CEOs fly from one meeting to another throughout their busy days. Often there's simply no time to prepare adequately for a meeting. They rely on those attending to brief them on the fly.

This strategy wastes not only your time, but also that of your people. They must bring you up to speed on the latest developments of the topic. That takes time. By default, you have placed yourself in the compromising position of having to take their word for assumptions that might be dead wrong. Finally, you have given yourself zero time to think about your various options and the downstream effects of selecting one over another.

It's much better to do a little homework before each meeting. First, determine the purpose of the meeting and the result you want from it. Then develop your own agenda that achieves your desired result. Take a few moments by yourself to assess the attendees. Understand their likely position (for or against particular courses of action) and why they might feel that way. Strategize how best to move them over to your position.

Meeting dynamics

Most meetings—especially those making high-stakes decisions—are a competition. The attendees are each trying to sell their position and get what they want or as much of it as they can. Those who arrive unprepared or feel things might go against them, may try hijacking the meeting. They do this by substituting a different topic and claim it is far more important than the one originally assigned to this meeting. Naturally, they are the only one prepared to discuss this new topic. If allowed to continue with such an ambush, they will wrestle control of the entire meeting over to themselves. They immediately jump from being the least prepared to the only one with something valid to contribute. They win by forfeit.

There is a way to stop such hijackers. Having your own written agenda including each topic, purpose, and the decisions to be made or the work product at the end establishes who is in control. It's much more difficult to wrestle control away from someone who is prepared and aware of the latest developments on the topic. Nevertheless, it won't stop the most determined hijackers from trying.

Before they can get rolling on the reasons why you must change the meeting purpose, stop them. However you do it, be sure to seize the floor. Do not let them argue their case by asking why they think theirs is the more important mission.

One tactic is to solicit peer pressure by asking the group if the hijacker's new topic has a higher priority than what everyone came here to discuss in the first place. Of course, you want the group to speak as one against the hijacker. It just might work. However, this tactic is not without some risk. Be sensitive to the group's dynamics. The hijacker just may have sufficient influence over the group that no one is about to disagree with her. Like any good lawyer, never ask a question whose answer you don't already know. If you get the wrong answer, you'll be in a worse position than when you started and you'll only have yourself to blame.

Alternatively, you might, say something like:

"I understand why you think we need to put topic A ahead of topic B. I appreciate your concern. I've thought about just that thing. You and I are on the same page and share the big picture. We have the same cause and purpose. My approach and priorities are a little different from yours right now, but in the end we'll finish together. This is my agenda for this meeting. If you want to talk about something else, let's talk offline when this is over and the issue is resolved. But for now, I need your thoughts and insight on topic B. Can I count on you?"

When facing a CEO who is so politely adamant about not allowing the obvious hijacking to proceed, there is little the perpetrator can do. The final question, *"Can I count on you"*, forces the perp to climb on board.

Selecting the meeting venue

Make no mistake, for high-stakes meetings and conversations the proper venue contributes mightily to your success. Consider the nuances and relative power positions of the various venues. For example, meeting on your home turf gives you significant power. The meeting is coming to you by your command. It might be in your personal conference room or your boardroom. For very high-stakes meetings, there is no more significant seat of power than your personal office.

Conversely, if your mission is to have an open dialog and to solicit the advice of your team, choose a venue that levels the playing field. It could be a conference room (not at your exclusive level) in the department that is championing the decision. Certainly, high-stakes conversations that are difficult or have an emotional component—such as disciplining someone—should be face-to-face.

For those conversations that are more collaborative or process related, you might want to substitute a telephonic conference call. Depending on the team's familiarity with one another, you may choose a video conference call such as the service offered by Skype Video. Be sure to set up the mechanics of the call well ahead of time.

When you choose a conference call, be aware that this venue also comes with some risks. First, people tend to multitask when on the telephone. Adding a video component cuts down on that. But remember, people can always turn their video on and off. Just know that when someone opts out of the video portion, their attention has wandered or perhaps they have even left the call entirely.

To keep people engaged when on a conference call, be sure to call on them. Ask their opinion or if they agree with what's being said. Invite them into the conversation.

Three stages of meetings

A CEO's Secret Weapon

There are three meeting parts vital to achieving meaningful results for any meeting. The first is your preparation before the meeting. Decide if it's worth having the meeting at all. Could you achieve the same results some other, less time intensive way? If the problem is personnel related and has been going on for a while, the answer is probably not.

The second vital stage of a meeting turns on how you conduct it. If you are delivering bad news and still want to maintain a valuable working relationship afterwards, then immediately set the person at ease. For example, opening with, *"John, we have to talk..."* puts the other person on high alert. Suddenly they are wondering what is wrong and beginning to put up their defenses to deflect any assault they know must surely be coming their way. A better way to open a conversation that makes the person more comfortable is something like, *"Pam, we have a good working relationship. You're a solid contributor. When we end this conversation, we're going to be in an even better position to move forward"*. See the difference? The more gentle opening stops Pam's imagination from running wild, wondering what anvil you're about to drop on her head. She's not thinking about her worst fears, as is John in the first example. Pam can listen. If no one listens to what we have to say, then nothing we say matters.

The third stage of a meeting is the post-meeting follow-up. During the meeting, you probably created an action plan to accomplish what you decided to do in the meeting or to implement whatever decisions were made. Following-up allows you to confirm your understanding of what is expected of each attendee by verbally stating or writing down the expectations. Name the individuals responsible and set deadlines with real dates. Hold the people accountable for delivering on the promises they made in the meeting. A few days before the deadlines (if you're not closely

68

monitoring progress more frequently) check with each person to be sure they'll deliver on their promises on time.

PowerPoint presentations

Microsoft's PowerPoint software has been hugely successful. It seems every meeting uses some sort of automated presentation software if not PowerPoint, then a lookalike. There are pros and cons to using it. To some, it's distracting and draws attention away from the speaker. Some speakers use it as a crutch, reading their entire presentation right from the screen.

The smartest people I've seen use presentation graphic software only when *preparing* for their meeting. They probably won't actually use it at the meeting. Instead, the *process* of creating a logical argument supported by facts and images is the real value; they then have a case with a beginning, middle and an end. It is logical and well thought out. All you need to do now is present your case. The pretty presentation graphics won't enhance what you have to say any more than your polished delivery.

If you do have to use presentation graphics in making your point, consider some rules when preparing your presentation:

- o **Order of the slides**: Put your slides in an order that logically flows from one major point to another. Don't force your audience to jump around, trying to piece together disjointed logic.
- o **Always include handouts** of the slides when you make a presentation. Give them out before you get started so people can make notes of your comments on each slide in real time.
- o **Hook your audience** with the first slide. Usually this answers the question on everyone's tongue: *What's in it for me?* Tell them. If your explanation convinces

them why they should listen to you, the presentation will go that much smoother.
- **Limit the key takeaway points** in the presentation to no more than three. More than that and people will forget.
- **Stick to generalities on the slides**. You can speak to the details. That's why you're there. Moreover, in a few seconds they can read the general slide and return their attention to you.
- **No bullet point should be longer than a few words**—four or five words are optimum.
- **No slide should have more than four bullet points**. Be sure to balance the bullets with images, graphs and other visuals that cement your point.
- **Keep the number of slides you use to a minimum**. Plan to talk for at least five minutes per slide. So if you're making a 20-minute presentation, limit yourself to four or five slides. You are the attraction, not the graphic presentation.

The cost of non-productive meetings

A meeting that accomplishes nothing wastes everyone's time. But the carnage doesn't stop there. The meeting was held to do something—perhaps make a needed decision. By not reaching a conclusion, no decision is made and the cost in manpower, machine time and the possible loss of competitive advantage can run into huge numbers. That's an opportunity cost.

Some enterprises replace decision-making with having meetings that never resolve anything. To them, such analysis paralysis is the most conservative approach. The devil they know is better than the devil they don't know. These organizations and the CEO's who aid and abet such behavior are destined for at best a mediocre performance. They will never be the lead dog and their view will never change.

Timing high-stakes conversations

The standard time allotted to a meeting having any importance seems to be one hour. We could be talking about seating arrangements at the board's quarterly meeting or acquiring the company that just mastered cold fusion. The time would be the same—one hour.

The fact is, meetings will fill the time allotted. The supporting discussion and presentation of facts usually takes 45-50 minutes. Making the final decision takes the last 10-15 minutes. If we were to compress the allotted time by half, the proportions would be the same. The same decision would still be made. However, a lot of the posturing, positioning and the arguing just to let people know you are present would be abbreviated or eliminated.

Compressing the time allotted to meetings gets rid of the fluff. What you're left with is the unadorned issue, only the arguments for and against and the final decision. Try cutting the allotted meeting time by half and see what happens.

How much is enough time?

There's a corollary to deliberately compressing allotted meeting times. That is, taking enough time to discuss options, reach a conclusion and assign tasks and accountability. What if the allotted time isn't enough? While this doesn't often happen if you've trained your staff to stick with what matters and prioritize the conversation, you may find the minute timer run out of sand. What do you do?

Stopping the meeting in favor of reconvening later could stop the momentum achieved. On the other hand, it could also give people a chance to think about the progress and why it occurred. When the meeting is reconvened, the participants are refreshed and ready to move on at a faster pace.

Everyone has their opinions about stopping a meeting that runs over the allotted time or keeping it going. I can tell you that my own opinion is to stop and summarize the progress. Make task assignments and schedule the next meeting at the very earliest possible date for an allotted time of half that of the first meeting. During the intervening time, as CEO, I speak with each participant and unearth any concerns or worries they might have but didn't get the time to voice. When the meeting reconvenes, I speak on their behalf, stopping frequently to ask if I have correctly stated their case. We move right through the agenda to the decision point. When it comes time to make the decision, we do not hesitate.

When deciding how much time to allocate to meetings, opt for the shortest possible time. Insist that the participants arrive briefed on the issues, well informed and ready to participate. The first such short-time meeting may be difficult because people are used to a less urgent, more social structure. They can learn to work with a more decisive structure.

Once the shortened meeting is working, everyone is being heard, and effective decisions are being made, shorten the allotted time again. The intent is to ratchet down the time allotted to every meeting. Your people will learn that the real decisions are actually engineered and negotiated outside the meeting. The meeting simply presents the decisions to which all the key players have already agreed.

An Alternative Meeting Option

For quick, high impact meetings to align everyone's priorities, consider the Stand Up Meeting. All participants stand in a circle and share their daily objectives. The meeting lasts 5 minutes times the number of people, and then everyone goes back to work without duplication of efforts and clarity of purpose.

Shaping Perception

High-stakes conversations focus on what really matters. What's important, however, is a matter of perception. As CEO, your job is to persuade and shape that perception so that everyone shares the same cause and purpose and moves ahead as a single entity.

A person's perception begins the instant they walk into the place where the high-stakes conversation is taking place. They attach meaning to everything including if the counterparty to this high-stakes conversation is on time.

Being late sends a message just as surely as does being early. How are they dressed? A business suit commands authority whereas the polo shirt and khaki pants of the engineering department says you're there to listen to new ideas. Does the person leave their jacket on or take it off and loosen their tie? Again, these actions and choices—whether deliberate or accidental—send a message before anyone has said a thing.

Entire books have been written about the messages that seating arrangements send—not to mention the shape of the table. The power positions seem to be the head of the table or the exact middle. My opinion is that seating CEOs in the middle of the table sends the message that they are a listener and arbitrator rather than referee as the head position implies.

 Whom you chose to sit next to is important. That person should be either your strongest ally or the enemy you want to keep close. The point is to be conscious and intentional about everything in order to shape people's perceptions the way you want.

A working model for conducting a high stakes conversation

Organizations lose a considerable percentage of their operating performance because their managers cannot step up and master crucial confrontations. Effectively, conducting high stakes conversations is a learned skill. There is nothing wrong with confrontation. However, it does require a few simple rules:

Emotion is the chain saw to constructive conversation. Make sure that everyone understands to keep emotion out of it.
The conversation is conducted with respect and kept at a conversational volume. There is no shouting and screaming. What takes place during such conversations stays there. This is not for public consumption.

Preparing for a high stakes conversation

First, decide just what a high stakes conversation is. If you're the CEO or a highly placed manager at an enterprise, what your subordinates perceive as high stakes may not be to you. After all, you have to consider issues far beyond single departments or even what happens within the company. Your perspective is global in nature.

Nevertheless, if your subordinate perceives this as a high stakes conversation, you had better treat it with equal importance. Anything less sends the very negative message that the individual isn't nearly as important to you as she thinks.

Your mission in having a conversation to resolve a conflict is simple: Resolve the problem and at the same time improve the motivation and relationship. Accomplishing that requires honesty on both sides and maybe sharing a little bit more of yourself than you usually do before large groups. There's nothing wrong with letting the counterparty to this conversation feel that you have opened up to him. He will feel special. Special is good—it generates loyalty. It says that you entrusted him with something that not everyone knows about you.

The tables could even turn if you, as CEO, are having a conflict resolution conversation with one of your company's opinion leaders. These special people have considerable influence over their colleagues. They generally aren't reluctant to hold both co-workers and their bosses accountable for mistakes. Imagine how you would conduct such a conversation with a thought leader who demanded to talk with you because she thinks you screwed up. This person just called *you* out on the carpet. What do you do?

Be respectful. Imagine what it took to demand such a conversation. Listen carefully. Acknowledge their points. However, never, ever forget who is boss. Equally as important, make sure that both of you don't lose sight of the cause, purpose and *Why* of you both being there. Resolve the problem and end with a better relationship than with which you began the conversation.

Sticking to what matters

Identify the desired result before the conversation takes place. Be detailed. There should be a number of takeaways from this conversation. Focus on the content and the relationship with this individual after the conversation. Once you have these things in mind, stick to them.

If you find yourself giving reasons why this conversation doesn't need to take place, take a moment. Ask yourself if you're afraid of losing the confrontation? What are the risks? Conversely, what are the effects and the risk of *not* having the conversation? There is an upside and downside to everything.

Put yourself in the counterparty's shoes. For example, if they failed to deliver on a promise they made, ask yourself why. What role could you have played to make the outcome more positive?

Do not see this person as a villain or a failure. If their record up until this time was good, then you're just dealing with a temporary stumble or an unexplained lapse of judgment. Its cause might even have nothing whatsoever to do with work. Perhaps there are personal issues—a divorce, or a sick child—that distracted him. It is your responsibility to find out, to care and to fix it.

Begin the conversation by stating the facts. Describe the performance gap between what was promised and what was delivered. Keep it unemotional. Be sure your facts are correct and indisputable, and then move on to diagnose what the problem was that created the gap. Give the counterparty ample opportunity to participate in the conversation.

Reach an agreement about what happened and why. Then devise a plan to repair what damage this performance gap caused and to ensure it doesn't occur again. Part of this conversation is also to identify potential barriers to success and figure out how to surmount them.

Dealing with deflection

Some people are afraid to admit fault. Perhaps they fear the loss of their job or their status within the organization. It could be their ego forbids them admitting anything less than being an expert in all things. They will try deflecting the blame or changing the topic. They offer excuse after excuse. They will bring up new potential problems far more serious than the original one. What to do?

Weigh the issue, keeping in mind what brought you both to this point in the first place. Is it in fact legitimately more serious? Is it more time-sensitive than the original topic? Probably not. If it were, you'd be aware of it long before now. Be flexible, but don't allow yourself to be sidetracked to a lesser issue by a habitual deflector.

High stakes conversations with the best qualified participants

Everyone wants an audience with the CEO and her senior executives. There's prestige in that. As CEO, you have only so much time. Identify the highest of the high stakes conversations in which you absolutely must be involved. Next, identify those people best qualified to participate in order to resolve the issue and further the cause, purpose and *Why*.

Keep in mind that the right person is not necessarily the one who agrees with you. Indeed, those who disagree can often offer insight of which you were perhaps unaware. Listen to these dissidents. Even if you still disagree with them after listening closely to their arguments, the conversation presents the rare opportunity to convert them to your way of thinking. Often the newly converted become the most vigorous advocates of their new religion.

Failing to seek out the high stakes conversations in favor of the easier, less crucial ones, is the same as abstaining from making the tough decisions. CEOs who habitually take the easy road rarely hang on to their jobs for long. People lose their faith and trust in such non-leaders.

Conversely, CEOs who create safe communications channels, no matter how difficult the topic, garner respect and trust. Their open door is much more than a high ideal—it is actually an open mind. It is reality in the truest sense. Certainly difficult conversations expend far more energy than any other type. However, they are usually the most productive in terms of decision making, forming alliances, and gathering support where adversaries once existed. This actually saves energy in the long run by avoiding wrong decisions.

Finally, since those former dissidents have now been pulled into the mainstream conversation, you have ratcheted up their stake in the outcome. They're now more motivated than ever before.

* * *

Chapter 5: Staying Positive under Fire: What are you thinking?

Effective leadership happens when things go wrong. Suddenly everyone is looking at you, the CEO, for direction. What happens next can often mean the difference between success and failure. CEOs who suddenly find themselves under fire need to adopt the leadership style needed in the moment. During crises, that's usually *conscious leadership*—that is, leading with a definite cause and *Why* in mind. The leader is conscious of her reactions that will dictate how everyone responds.

A leader who panics will elicit like kind panic throughout the company. People don't even have to observe panic. For example, say the financial media is predicting a downgrade in the credit ratings of a company's bonds. The CEO barricaded himself in his office with no outgoing communications to manage the press. Keeping the employees informed is not even a thought. Chances are he's unnerved, frightened and probably doesn't know what to do. That sends a clear message (the wrong message, but definitely a clear one) to all concerned about their jobs.

Then there's the *command and control* leadership style. We typically find this in older leaders, used to an authoritarian regime or in very young, inexperienced CEOs who aren't confident enough to accept help. Command and control means there's just one person in command and he is in complete, undisputed control. Right or wrong, the C&C leader will make all the decisions. This leader has effectively asked the employees to trust his ability and his alone to extricate the company from the crisis.

The natural question that employees, board members, investors, creditors, customers and lenders will ask of a C&C leader is, *does this individual have what it will take to get out of this mess?* Military organizations are famous for their C&C leadership style—with good reason. When things go wrong, decisions need to come fast and from experienced hands. The battlefield is no place for a collegial management style.

However, with some notable exceptions—the securities industry, for one— the business world is not the battlefield. Indeed, for some industries the best leadership style during times of crisis is the *servant leader*. The CEO takes on the job of clearing the way for the managers to do what's necessary to defuse the crisis. This is the type of CEO who can pick up the telephone and order a reluctant vendor to ship the critical part immediately or—by God—they will never see another order from this company or any of its subsidiaries again.

Emotional intelligence

The ability to identify, assess, and control your own emotions and those of others and groups, is a necessary skill for CEOs who must lead under adverse conditions. Emotional intelligence (EQ) requires the CEO to control their feelings and emotions when under fire. This doesn't mean just showing an outward appearance of calm while your stomach is doing back flips. Instead, you must harness your emotions and channel them to create a constructive solution.

People can see through a CEO who is bravely trying to keep a stiff upper lip. Soon that lip will quiver. When it does, people's trust and confidence will deteriorate quickly. Use your powers of emotional intelligence to relate to your constituency. Your job while under fire is to inspire those around you to find and implement a solution.

Harnessing EQ means that you work to rekindle people's passion and enthusiasm for the overall cause, purpose and *Why*. Keep them committed and motivated. Adversity creates a fertile atmosphere for intense bonding. It's true that the deepest friendships are those forged in battle. Why? Because everyone is suffering equally, working for a common cause, and against a common enemy. These are strong motivators. It is part of the success of the company, Outward Bound. There, they deliberately put participants in risky and adverse situations that force them to rely on one another.

A CEO with a highly developed sense of emotional intelligence—their own, as well as the group's—can utilize adversity to accelerate change beyond what it would have been under more normal circumstances.

The art of primal leadership

This leadership style appeals to people's emotions. Let's face it; adversity certainly creates an emotional response. Employees fear for their jobs. Lenders worry that their loans may default. Customers are anxious that their critical order may be delayed. Investors wring their hands over a possible drop in the yield of their venture.

Leaders who create the proper emotional response can guarantee that everything else they do will work as well as it possibly can. The wrong moods and actions (or inactions) can poison the emotional climate of the workplace. The leader's perception of a crisis carries huge weight. It governs the way the entire company perceives events even in the face of chaos.

Great leaders move their people. Great leadership works through people's emotions. Leaders who fail to drive emotions in the right direction will not be nearly as effective in working through the crisis *du jour*.

It begins with the mood and tone in which they deliver the message. The effective leader who has properly gauged the group's EQ will dial in the emotional impact of what they say and do. They will seek to raise morale and commitment especially in the face of adversity.

A good example of using EQ to motivate people to a higher cause took place in a number of industries right after the 911 attacks. The CEOs suddenly turned their attention outward, against a common enemy. So did the employees. They bonded on a mission that was suddenly larger than anything they could ever do individually. As a coordinated team, they became a formidable force. More than a few American flags hung from the rafters of manufacturing facilities. For those companies involved in manufacturing the V-hulled bomb-resistant vehicles used by our troops in Iraq and Afghanistan, their cause and purpose was clear: Protect our boys and bring them home safely.

Their cause and purpose had not changed. The *Why* never changes. However, there was a new sense of urgency. Suddenly a common enemy existed; now he had a face and a name.

Managing the meaning of the issue

The CEO has the power to set the meaning of a *dynamic incident* or a *fluid situation* or just a plain crisis. Call it whatever you wish—it's a problem. The leader has the ability to put the issue in perspective. Certainly, people will begin doing that for themselves. However, only the CEO has the global reach and vision to put it in its *overall* perspective. The CEO's interpretation of the crisis resonates and filters throughout the organization.

Of course, the CEO's interpretation must stand up to scrutiny. It cannot be viewed as uninformed or naïve. It is the CEO's correct interpretation of the problem that gives people the courage to prevail when things don't go their way. That interpretation must be consistent with the organization's cause, purpose and *Why*.

An example occurred in a huge medical practice. The largest patient insurance provider booted them out of the PPO plan because they refused to accept a larger discount in their fee payments when their contract came up for renewal. Suddenly, the medical corporation's CEO faced a potentially devastating loss of 45 percent of its revenue. Employees were nervous. Long standing patients began leaving for other doctors who were in the insurance company's PPO plan.

What did the CEO do? She didn't panic. She held a town hall meeting with all employees. She told them honestly what had happened, why she made the decision she had and what it meant to the company in revenue loss. She also put forth an idea. She asked the question, "What would you say if I told you that there's a way to use this circumstance to reduce our workload, give our remaining patients better medical care than they ever thought possible *and* to increase our profits?"

Of course, this question was met with some skepticism. After all, traditionally such huge practices were dependent on the revenue from the large insurance companies. Nevertheless, the CEO persevered because she stuck to her cause, purpose and her *Why*—giving patients the very best medical care the current state of the art allowed.

She told the employees her plan. It involved a good deal of honest communication with the patients. It required reassignment and retraining of over 20 people whose jobs revolved around insurance billing and collections. No, the company would no longer accept insurance claims in lieu of payment from patients. However, it would have all the claim forms available for the patients themselves to seek *reimbursement* for professional fees paid when delivered.

Requiring payment for services rendered when performed was a novel concept. The CEO hired Los Angeles based Writers

Resource Group, Inc. to craft the announcement sent to the patients. This critical communication presented the issue and the impact on the patients fairly, honestly and in plain English, something for which WRG is justifiably famous.

The company did indeed lose some patients. It amounted to a reduction of about 5 percent in revenue. The CEO anticipated that loss—actually she expected it to be more like 10 percent. Operating expenses decreased by about 20 percent. Because profit margins rose, the doctors no longer had to shove through a minimum of 50 patients each per day just to break even. Indeed, the minimum daily patients seen by each doctor dropped by one third. They could take the time needed to raise the quality of care they provided. The CEO communicated these results to the employees in another town hall meeting.

Word got around that this was a different kind of medical practice. Doctor visits began with the doctor walking into the waiting room to greet her patient and invite them into her office to first talk about the problem. Yes, it was indeed more expensive even after insurance reimbursement. But most patients agreed it was worth the extra cost.

The practice began growing again, but this time with patients willing to pay a premium for superior medical attention. Patients found that they received their reimbursement checks from the insurance company within 30 days anyway.

Why this strategy worked

This CEO took what appeared as a crisis to many and turned it into the opportunity of everyone's professional lives. Suddenly, everyone in this huge practice was providing the very best medical care available. The company was no longer a patient mill, grinding people through so it could bill an insurance company, regardless of patient outcome. The CEO correctly gauged and managed the emotional intelligence surrounding the crisis. She did indeed stay positive under fire.

Her steadfast adherence to the company's purpose—provide the best medical care available—was unwavering. It went beyond just keeping the company running and shoving sick bodies through its system like a factory. People saw that. Where once they felt that they worked in a huge medical bureaucracy where patients were simply cases, now they had the time and mandate to really treat them as human beings. The employees loved that—it was why they entered the profession in the first place. **The CEO gave them back their professional pride.**

This CEO's strategy worked because everything she did from first refusing to renew an onerous contract had a strategic purpose. Was it premeditated? You bet. Then again, so was the organization's cause and purpose.

The outcome was successful because the CEO and senior executives did not immediately react to the insurance company's demand with the first thing out of their mouths. Instead, they did some thinking. The CEO led the way, using the organization's cause and purpose as a guide. They ran the numbers and developed a plan.

Next, the CEO acknowledged and faced the rumors flying around the company of massive layoffs and possible bankruptcy. She managed her fears as well as everyone else's. During her two town hall meetings, she was honest. She didn't try to sugar coat the potentially dangerous course she had plotted. She reminded everyone of two things: Why they entered the medical profession and what the true purpose was of the company they joined.

She asked, "Who here is thrilled to be shoving people through a medical factory just to bill an insurance company?" Then she waited while everyone thought about that question. "Wouldn't you rather spend the time needed with a patient to get to the bottom of their problem and determine a course of treatment that will actually cure them? And then actually cure them?" The CEO stopped talking. The town hall meeting was quiet as everyone pondered this novel idea of practicing medicine—curing people rather than simply running tests to bill an insurance company. Could it work, they wondered.

"It will work," said the CEO, "Here's how…" And she outlined her plan to change the way the company did business. The change, by the way, was completely consistent with the organization's cause, purpose and *Why*—to provide the very best medical treatment available.

The next thing the CEO did that guaranteed success of her plan was to become transparent. She answered all questions. She openly discussed the company's revenues and expenses throughout the implementation of her plan. At first people saw revenues dip. "That's a lot less than we were expecting," said the CEO. "We're actually ahead of schedule."

This firm grasp of the financial controls immediately calmed the employees. Their first concern—understandably—was their paycheck. With that worry out of the way, their next question was, "How can I help?" Such openness about the finances did something else—it stopped people's vivid imaginations and speculation about going bankrupt. Financial security was no longer an issue.

The transparency this CEO insisted on gave people some skin in the game. They were a trusted and integral part of this reengineering of a huge healthcare delivery company. Suddenly, they were working for something much more significant than a paycheck.

This was a savvy CEO. She understood that it couldn't be just about money. She knew the people were curious to see if such a sea change was possible. She also knew that they wanted to feel the pride they once had in helping sick people actually get better. How did she know these things? She felt them herself. That's how every successful leader works—by placing themselves in their people's shoes and vice versa.

Conscious Leadership

Conscious leaders choose the right leadership style for the situation at hand. This is just a fancy way of saying that leaders must manage their own emotions in order to direct others. The CEO's perception and reaction to events sets the tone. When under fire, this is a difficult task; nevertheless, correctly assessing the impact of the issue both currently and into the future is essential. The effect varies depending on the audience. Employees, for example, want to know how it will affect their job, their upward mobility, their upcoming salary raise and their retirement plan.

Let's say your manufacturing plant suddenly burns to the ground. Your customers will want to know just how you intend to get them their critical parts. Your vendors have the opposite reaction. They had a boatload of inventory in that plant that burned down. To them, that translates into accounts receivable. How does this disaster affect your cash flow and ability to pay outstanding invoices?

When crises like the one in our example and others occur, the list of people affected by your company expands past your customers and vendors. One of the most important is the surrounding community. If the crisis is of a physical nature—such as if one of your company's locomotives pulling a train load of toxic chemicals becomes a runaway along a rail line spanning three states—the definition of *surrounding community* becomes immense. Would a situation like this test your abilities to manage your own emotions? Absolutely.

No matter the crisis, it's important to remember that how you react resonates and filters down to each constituency. It is up to the leader to give people the courage to prevail when things aren't going their way.

Foundations of emotional intelligence

The most effective crisis managers are the ones who have learned how to deal with adversity well before they need the skill. Most large companies with corporate communications departments hold periodic crisis management drills. These teach everyone what to do, how to do it and who is responsible. They give a boost to everyone's confidence in being able to deal with a crisis since they've already practiced it a number of times.

For the CEO, crisis management hinges on the four platforms of emotional intelligence:

- Self-awareness
- Self-management
- Social awareness
- Relationship management
-

Self-awareness

This is the most basic EQ skill every leader needs. Understand what external stimulus causes which emotions. Once you know that, then you're in a position to do something about it. Chances are your audience will have much the same emotional reaction to the same stimulus. Leaders who understand how others feel can tune in and adjust their message to keep it in harmony with the circumstances, the over arching cause and the purpose.

Leaders who are aware of their own emotions keep their values, goals and *Why* in the forefront always. They have an understanding of their emotions along with their personal strengths and limitations. Knowing these things helps plot the course with the highest likelihood of success.

The decisions made to deal with a crisis—to stay cool under fire—are well thought out. Such leaders know where they're headed and why. That never changes. The crisis just represents a temporary diversion and series of actions that remain consistent with the over arching cause.

Leaders with good self-awareness possess the ability to look beyond the immediate situation. They understand how to deal with the current problem. What's more difficult is managing the impact that sits over the horizon, beyond view. Plotting their course of action most definitely sets up the things they will need to do once they solve the immediate problem to manage the future impact.

This requires the skill to look beyond the data. Develop a macro viewpoint. Think of a dam bursting in a small town. The town is immediately flooded. The first necessity is getting the residents to high ground so no one drowns. Next, provide for their physical needs until the dam is shored up and the floodwaters recede.

However, while this is going on, the CEO of the electrical utility that owns the dam and is responsible for its failure is looking down stream. There are thousands of acres of crops that will soon be underwater and ruined. Beyond that, the price of these commodities will rise as they become in scarce supply over the next twelve months. Then there are the farmers and their families whom the dam just put out of business for a time. This CEO has a responsibility to each constituency.

Qualities of a self-aware leader

It's easy to list the qualities I've seen in the most successful leaders. These all usually filter down to how well they know themselves and the cause to which they have committed. However, these ideals are not always so easy to live up to—especially during times of crisis.

A CEO and leader of a company who openly discloses his true purpose and *Why* **is transparent to those around him**. This is a good thing. Generally, these values further the lives and circumstances of others. Remember the Wright Brothers earlier? They just wanted to achieve manned flight for the good of mankind. They were easy to see through. Langley, however, wanted to use the achievement of manned flight for self-promotion and personal enrichment. The public never saw his real agenda.

The only way to lead an organization through a fluid and dynamic situation is to adapt your actions as events unfold. Your goal and purpose never changes, just how you get there. **Adaptable leaders are comfortable with life's ambiguities.** They don't waste time fretting and worrying about the unfairness of it all. They accept the situation, and then find a way to either neutralize its effects on their journey or reroute their course around it.

The CEO's steadfast commitment to cause and purpose serves as a compass. Adversity fills business life every day of the week. If it's not the unions, it's the customers. If not the customers, it's the suppliers. Don't get me started on the competitors. They are always trying to get a leg up on your company. The point is that you deal with each one, get around it and continue on your way toward your goal.

That's how an effective CEO controls her own destiny—by seeing the opportunities in the challenges she faces. Earlier I described the bankruptcy of a critical supplier and what the manufacturing manager was going to do about it. **Opportunities are buried in one's perspective**. Where the manager saw no way out, the CEO saw the break he was looking for. He got into the supplier's business for pennies on the dollar and vertically integrated his supply chain. Suddenly he had a reliable supplier (because he now owned the company) and complete control over the parts' quality.

Effectively managing your reactions and emotional surges in the middle of adversity does something very important; it shoves the clutter out of the way and allows you to deal with just the situation at hand. Emotions erupting in a dynamic situation can imprison people. It's the deer-in-the-headlight syndrome—you can't move, let alone make a reasoned decision. The CEO who has mastered her emotions can move quickly and decisively. Her intent is to get out ahead of the evolving situation and seize control over it. When people portray a leader as the one to have at your side when the shooting starts, that's the type of individual they're describing.

Self management skills

The US Navy SEALs have a motto: *It pays to win.* For the SEALs winning is often a matter of life and death, but for most CEOs winning is not so serious. Nevertheless, both the SEALs and the CEO have one thing in common: In order to win, each must have extraordinarily strong self-management skills. The CEO must prove himself worthy of the trust his people place in him every day. A series of missteps will begin to erode that trust. Soon, his qualifications to lead will be questioned.

Think of a married political candidate who has a romantic affair with a young campaign staffer. A child results from the union. That's bad. However, what makes matters even worse is the cover-up afterwards, the lying and subterfuge to try to maintain the candidate's fragile public image as a man of principal and unwavering ethics.

Obviously, the public becomes aware that this individual has no self-management skills whatsoever. We all know intuitively, that without such skills, no person is qualified to hold the office of President of the United States. The job requires handling crisis after crisis, day in and day out. One is more serious than the next. The inability to control one's emotions and visceral reactions would drive that person insane. When the electorate is evaluating its political candidates, you can bet emotional control is at the top of the list of qualifications we're all looking for.

Integrity means living your values

Effective leadership demands the ability to manage feelings— yours as well as your constituents'. Great leaders can express their feelings with conviction. They are consistent in the application of their personal values over every situation. This consistency of integrity, values and purpose generates trust. There is a confidence in someone whose reactions to adversity are predictable.

How often have you heard someone say, "I know her. She would never do that. It's just the way she's built; such integrity is in her DNA." This person would follow such integrity to the very end. Compare that with, "The guy's a loose canon. Who knows what he'll do. I'd like to think he'd put the investor's interests before his own, but who knows?"

Leaders move people by authentically sharing their dream. It is their cause, their purpose and their *Why*. As their positive vision spreads, the group rallies around a common goal. Effective leaders articulate this shared mission. Their consistency of purpose and the integrity with which they execute decisions allows people to join in and follow.

You CAN Teach Old Leaders New Tricks

The ability to inspire and motivate people with a compelling vision is the most effective tool in any leader's toolbox. Such inspirational leaders excite people about following their vision because they are aware of their own guiding principles. They can effectively articulate them. During trying times, these principles always surface as a beacon. We refer to these guiding principles as *"Hows"*.

Some CEO's have been the boss for way too long. They've seen it all. They have lost their enthusiasm for the business and its mission. They're bored. This trickles down throughout the company. It's true that people take on the attitude and demeanor of the boss; if the boss has no fun at the company, neither will they. It becomes just a job with a paycheck and such jobs are fungible—one is just like another. Any loyalty that people may have had to the company and the boss is soon lost.

Reigniting enthusiasm

Enthusiasm begins at the top. Is it possible to teach an old boss, new tricks? It is. One person transmits the signals, it then intermingles with others. Soon emotions spread irresistibly when people work together for a common purpose. The more cohesive the group, the stronger the feeling of commonality. The CEO can ignite such enthusiasm. Here's how: by spreading cheerfulness, warmth and the *Why*.

Cheerfulness and warmth spread the most easily of any feeling. Irritability is less contagious. After all, who wants to feel irritable? Depression is the least likely emotion to spread. It's not impossible. Still, who wants to exchange a cheerful demeanor for one that is dour?

The CEO absolutely must have a truly personal interest and passion in the organization's cause, purpose and *Why*. If he doesn't, he should not be at the helm of the ship. A new CEO who buys into the cause or creates a new one should be appointed. If the dour CEO is the owner, what do you do? Maybe he hates the job and isn't maximizing the enterprise's true capabilities. Perhaps he needs to embark on a new venture, one that has a cause in which he believes.

It happens more often than you think. Owner/CEOs have an epiphany. **Their company,** the company they built from scratch, is just marking time. Either they sell the business or they hire a professional CEO and start a new enterprise—perhaps a nonprofit—for which they have renewed enthusiasm.

Harnessing optimism

Optimism is generally inherent in human nature. Most people want to believe that things will get better. If the CEO believes it—truly believes it—chances are, so will the employees. Good moods influence how effectively people work together and cooperate for the common goal. Along with this come the ancillary benefits of fairness and the drive to improve performance.

People also naturally gravitate to laughter. We all want to see and hear what is so funny or why people are having more fun than we are. Laughter, and the smiles that go with it, are contagious. It can create a chain reaction that spreads quickly through a group. Suddenly the group is sharing an experience together, and sharing is good. It means people's hearts as well as their minds are coordinated. If it's the boss leading the joke, so much the better. Everyone wants to see their leader having fun. It gives permission for everyone else to enjoy their jobs. The boss's mood and attitude ripples throughout the organization.

A team will look to their leader's emotional reaction to gauge the gravity of a crisis. A good example is one of the greatest clutch drives in football history. It took place during the fourth quarter of the AFC Championship Game on January 11, 1987 between the Denver Broncos and the Cleveland Browns. While in the huddle on their own two-yard line, down by a touch down with five minutes and two seconds left to play Broncos offensive guard, Keith Bishop, said, "Alright guys, we got 'em right where we want 'em." Bishop's statement was so ridiculous that it cracked up everyone in the huddle. Broncos Quarterback, John Elway, took over from there. In those famous five minutes, he and his now loosened up team drove the ball 98 yards to tie the game with 37 seconds left in regulation. The Broncos won the game in overtime with a field goal, 23-20.

Bishop's colossal understatement of their dire situation and his inveterate optimism served to break the tension and loosen up the team. At that critical moment, Bishop became the leader his team needed and the others just followed along.

Optimistic leaders frame the group's mission in ways that enhance the meaning of each person's contribution. Their rejection of potential failure gives people a sense of clarity and direction. A leader who never considers anything but complete success sets his team free to use their best efforts and not worry about the consequences because they know their boss has their back.

The more a charismatic leader transmits her positive emotions to the group, the higher the likelihood it will spread. When it spreads, people naturally gravitate to her upbeat feelings. That's why emotionally intelligent leaders attract talented people who want to work in their presence.

The opposite is true as well. Domineering, cold leaders repel people. Their subordinates work for a paycheck rather than to support the cause.

Changing old habits

No matter how set in their ways a leader is, they can always change their methods to suit the situation. Dealing with the multiple generations now working in so many businesses is a good example. The command and control style of leadership (*I'm the boss and you'll do it my way or it's the highway for you*) simply does not work for the Gen-X'ers or the Millennials. They will rebel and laugh at such a didactic attitude.

The X'ers were born between 1961 and 1980. Their mission is to balance work with their personal lives. They are generally skeptical, self-reliant and willing to take a risk. A command and control boss will have to change to one who solicits ideas and recognizes their contribution to the team.

The Millennials are a different story entirely. These are the youngest members of the work force. They grew up in a nurturing generation where everyone is a winner. Each member of their last place soccer team gets a trophy. Their upbringing sheltered them from the realities of an otherwise tough, competitive world. The command and control boss who reads a Millennial the riot act about their work and who demands immediate improvement is liable to see them burst into tears. Their parents will then call to complain about such mistreatment and explain how hard the kid tries.

Whether the CEO has responsibility for X-ers, Millennials or just the Baby Boomers and Traditionalists (less so now since Traditionalists are rapidly retiring), their management style must be adjusted to fit the needs of their people. This is not selling out. This is just being an effective manager. You wouldn't try speaking French to a group who only understands English, would you? It's the same thing here.

The diversity of your workforce can bring incredibly new ideas. For example, Millennials are typically technology savvy. They grew up with video games and the latest in computers. Put them to work solving your tech-related issues. Since valuing change is also one of their endearing characteristics, they'll jump at the chance to be part of the next generation product.

CEOs must address yet another category of worker. They're more valuable than you can imagine. These are the Builders. Builders are often retired workers who for a variety of very good reasons have reentered the workforce. They bring a lifetime of experience with them to the job. Often Builders have seen the challenges you're facing right now and understand what works and what doesn't. Where you're getting on the job training, the builders quite likely have written the book. Seek out the Builder's wisdom. Learn from them.

Builders just want the respect that their experience and knowledge have earned them. A boss who gives them that will have an extraordinarily loyal and very smart group of followers.

New tricks for resolute leaders

Whatever you do as the leader will rub off on those around you. Your behavior becomes permission for others to behave the same way. CEO's who yell and scream at their subordinates will soon see a lot of similar yelling around the company.

If such behavior inhibits productivity (as it certainly will in departments populated by X-ers and Millennials), then change your own behavior. For example, leaders who do not make a conscious effort to curb their tendency toward rampant skepticism of any idea but their own will see the atmosphere of suspicion they have created. New ideas will lay dormant.

To change it, just make a conscious effort to be more accepting of others' opinions. You'll soon see more ideas flowing freely without fear of humiliation by skeptical supervisors trying to emulate the boss.

Some leaders—in fact many—are promoted to their leadership roles due to their technical expertise. Their superiors *hope* that they'll learn how to be effective leaders and managers. These people often struggle. For example, if a brilliant engineer is put in charge of satellite flight operations, she must transform out of the shy, quantitative nerd she once was. Her job now is to motivate and encourage the engineers—she was once a part of—to be creative and to get the job done on time.

If you're one of these neophyte leaders, one way to climb out of such a shell is to challenge yourself. Accept public speaking engagements. Write professional articles. Accept invitations from the press for interviews. Develop a personal brand of being visible and communicative in plain English rather than techno-babble.

You don't have to make this transition all at once, just try keeping one foot in the old persona and the other in the new brand of you. As you become more comfortable, extend a little more. Eventually, you'll make the complete transition out of the old persona.

There are few naturally born, gifted leaders, but most make themselves appear that way. Such leadership occurs where heart and mind, feelings and thought meet. Intellect alone does not make the leader. The best execute their vision by motivating, guiding, inspiring, listening, and persuading—all the while keeping one eye firmly fixed on the cause, purpose and *Why.*

Harnessing rituals

Everyone has certain rituals they go through. Watch a golfer prepare for a shot. They begin their ritual before ever touching the club. Fingers caress all the club heads, warm from the sun, while still in the bag. They settle on the one they want and pull it

A CEO's Secret Weapon

from the bag. Next, they address the ball with both feet together and gently set the club head a prescribed few millimeters behind the ball. The golfer stands there for a second, then both feet move apart and into the hitting stance. The club head lifts off the ground and waggles over the ball a very exact number of times. Now it comes back down behind the ball (but never touches the ground—to do so would require restarting this entire sequence). The backswing begins slowly at first, accelerating until it reaches the apex where the club is exactly parallel to the ground. At this point, the powerful downswing begins, gathering speed until the club head reaches maximum velocity just when it hits the ball. A golfer's ritual provides a familiarity and purpose in an often-unfamiliar setting—such as when the ball is behind a tree.

Like a golfer, a leader can use the rituals of decision making to huge advantage. For example, to maintain your focus and direction, review your vision for the company every day. Link it to your cause, purpose and Why. Share it with others. Think about how the most important things on your schedule today will move you closer to achieving your cause.

Another ritual is forcing your thoughts to stay on point rather than wondering. Such mental focus is difficult, especially when you're bored. Nevertheless, it reduces the amount of time spent spinning your wheels.

Create a ritual that refreshes you. Some CEO's will stop off at a park on the way home just to sit on a bench for a few minutes. It's like a diver coming to the surface. They need a decompression stop before they enter the dry world again. Perhaps this decompression ritual involves a spouse whose only job is to listen for ten minutes to anything you want to tell them. Such a time to blow off steam with someone you respect and who will not judge you is extraordinarily refreshing.

99

Some rituals actually give the CEO a break from being the boss. It's important to get out of the line of fire regularly. This gives the boss something to look forward to. Such a ritual break is especially important for a boss with workaholic tendencies. Most of us can get through anything just as long as we can see the light at the end of the tunnel. This respite is that light.

Chapter 6: "Assemble Your Who", talks about the assets you have all around you that can help you make critical decisions.

* * *

Chapter 6: Assemble Your WHOs: Tapping Resources

Whose counsel do you listen to? Many CEOs and business leaders have at least an informal group of wise and respected people from whom they seek advice. That's what we mean by your *Whos*.

If you are like many leaders, you employ several sources for advice depending on what you want to know. For matters affecting the company, its financial issues and investors, most turn to a statutory board of directors. For strategic and visionary issues that require issue-specific knowledge, your advisory board is probably a good bet. These boards are usually filled with experts that have broad and deep experience. For both types of issues, wise counsel is fairly easy to obtain.

Where do you turn for the more difficult, personal issues that keep every CEO awake at night? We're talking here about your *Why*, your cause and your purpose. These are things that most don't wish to share publicly while they're in the development stage. Once you've come to your conclusions, of course, your goals and decisions will become a matter of public record. But until then, many CEOs think they're on their own. That's a lonely road to walk.

Making good use of a trusted cadre of *Whos* adds a depth of understanding and insight that would otherwise be unavailable to most CEOs. For these special and intensely personal decisions, many CEOs seek advice from business coaches, their (non-competitive) industry peers, and some of their most trusted team members in the company who have a deep commitment to the *Why*, cause and purpose you both share.

Should I walk this path alone?

That depends. CEOs and leaders in general are a decisive, forward-leaning lot. They are paid to make decisions and, by God, they will make decisions.

These are the ones who believe no one can possibly understand the intricacies of the issues facing them. If they are going to listen to anyone's advice, that person had better know more than they do. So far they haven't found that person and they probably never will.

Often, the enterprise founders are solo leaders; when they started the company, they had no one but themselves to rely on. Things have worked out pretty well since then, so why change the formula for success? Because things change: Technology advances, markets expand and contract, and customers' requirements outgrow the vendor's capabilities that refuse to keep pace. That's the risk CEOs take who chose to exclude outside counsel from their decision making process.

Knowing when you need help

There are a number of tell tale symptoms that a CEO is suddenly at the limit of her capabilities and needs some help. First is the constant feeling of stress. Not surprising, since such insular individuals are constantly trying to reach beyond their grasp. They ask, "What's happening here? I never used to be at a loss?" Many CEOs under this cloud find themselves losing sleep at night. The hours of 1:00 a.m. to 3:00 a.m. (known far and wide as the *entrepreneur's hours)* find them wide awake and worrying about the business.

Another identifier of a problem is that their performance and that of their company seems to be standing still. That's because what once worked as an autocratic regime now requires answers and decisions that are beyond the autocrat's ability to provide. The

CEO is totally out of her comfort zone, but isn't willing to admit it. The enterprise is stuck. The employees know it, investors know it, and customers and vendors know it too. The only one who doesn't know it is the CEO. She listens to no one and seeks the advice of no one. She also has no one but herself to blame.

There is an answer: Admit that you could use a little expert advice, then go out and get it. Some leaders try hiring the advice. Often these senior advisors come in at the partner level or at least the executive VP level. Many receive the shiny new title of Head of Business Strategies. But really, they're the CEO's shrink.

Because of their senior status and the importance of their involvement, the leaders may give them a piece of the enterprise. This is very expensive advice, especially considering that such advice can be rented or engaged on a temporary consulting basis as needed and paid for in cash rather than in equity. But first, it requires admitting that you could make good use of it and can no longer analyze and implement every decision all by yourself.

Who do you know?

There's another vitally important aspect of knowing who your *Whos* are. When you are looking for help of almost any kind, whom do you know in your network of friends, relatives and business associates who can connect you to the right person or group of people?

I spoke at an event with "C" level people who were in transition. I was sharing the concept of how to find the people you need to know, when a hand shot up at the back of the room. A young man looking very distraught asked, "But what if I don't know anyone in Los Angeles? How do I make this concept work for me?" I expanded his whole universe with this simple but powerful lesson. He certainly knew people from St. Louis, where he came from. As a result, he reached out to everyone he knew there by asking: "I've just moved to Los Angeles and in an effort to meet quality people, I am asking you as someone I know and value who YOU know there that I should meet." This catapulted his results…all by asking his *Who's*.

Building a Solid Team

Even CEOs who have developed and use trusted advisory resources still need a trustworthy and levelheaded team. These are the people whom the CEO must trust to execute and implement their [now] well considered and informed decisions. Indeed, the internal team is often in on the CEO's decision making process. Their perspective is generally specific to the company and the impacts the decision will have on the business, its customers and its vendors.

All too often a new leader will inherit their predecessor's team. A group that once provided trusted counsel may not be appropriate for the successor leader. After all, there's a reason why the old leader is no longer there. It just might revolve around the decisions they made as a result of less-than-adequate advice received from their trusted team.

Additionally, things change. Causes, purposes and *Why's* might also change. If the old team members cannot get aboard with the new purpose, they are no longer the best people for the job.

Determining a good team member

Your inner circle of trusted team members should make things happen the way you want them to. However, building a trusted team is done one person at a time. There's a way to do it that will build an effective team. Stray from these principles and you'll create a disparate group that not only wastes your time, but creates a dissonance that is counter-productive to your mission.

When you are looking to identify who will make a good team member, first identify the qualities in a candidate that you know will help you take the organization to the next level. Your search for trusted team members shifts from subjective criterion to more quantitative. Develop a set of metrics against which you can assess the candidates' likelihood of success. Such attributes can be anything. For example, these are attributes that you might look for in a turnaround team:

- Decision making capabilities
- Track record of turnaround success
- Specific experience in turning around this type of organization or enterprise
- Trust
- Integrity
- Calm, clear thinking in the face of looming disaster
- Contacts in the communities you need such as technology, customers, vendors, lenders and investors
- Specialized skills needed on the team such as computer, finance, legal, manufacturing, logistics or engineering
- Fit into the team: This is a soft judgment. You want a team that gets along well enough so that personalities don't get in the way of execution. Keep in mind, though, you are not forming a group of best friends. The best team members challenge each other.
- The candidate must be in agreement with the cause, purpose and *Why*
- Ability to obtain buy-in: You need team members capable of selling others on decisions and obtaining their commitment.
- Confidence in their own abilities and the willingness to push back when they disagree

Example: Recruiting a benefactor

Let's say you run a nonprofit that requires a benefactor, or a for-profit like my own *Why Institute* for example (yes, this is a shameless plug as we would love to have a benefactor). The benefactor should be someone you wish to recruit into the team, not just for the money they might provide. The intent is that they become a valuable member of the CEO's advisory team as well. Along with some of the metrics listed above, what else might specifically qualify such a benefactor? Here are some specifics:

- Age: They may be elderly and ready to leave behind something when they're gone
- They regret that so far they have no legacy
- They have no children to carry on their work, ideals and special terests
- They want to leave their mark on the world
- They have $20 million in assets to bequeath
- They have a commitment (or at least an affinity) to your nonprofit's purpose, cause and *Why*.

Such specifics, when spelled out and combined with all the other metrics you're looking for, paint a vivid picture of the individual. As they say, if you don't know who you're looking for, anyone will do.

Finding your WHOs

Recruiting the individuals who meet the metrics listed above is not easy. Think of the process as putting many candidates into a funnel. The funnel measures their traits and capabilities against your metrics and just a few come out the bottom as viable candidates.

make a list of attributes I'm looking for

You will want to contact those people you know who could be useful in your recruiting effort. It doesn't matter if they are a candidate or not, they may know someone who is.

Getting to know your candidates

By this time, you've identified the qualities you are looking for in your team. You know everything about these people that you need to know except their names. That's coming now. It is time to begin assessing the candidates.

Assessment consists of fact gathering and confirming things you already know. On paper your short list of candidates appears to qualify. The personal interview assesses the accuracy of the paper description. Here are the points your interview must cover:

Prove the facts: Confirm the facts that your initial recruiting efforts uncovered. Ask penetrating questions to be sure the candidate's supposed capabilities and claimed experience actually exist.

Soft metrics: Assess compliance with the soft metrics such as how they fit with the team and their buy-in with the cause, purpose and *Why*. No matter how qualified the candidate, if they disrupt the team or don't align with the cause, purpose and *Why*, they won't contribute nearly what a somewhat less qualified, but better fitting candidate would. The latter will help the team achieve its goal.

Growth capability: Assess the candidate's ability to grow with the enterprise. This individual is a valued member of your inner team. You and the team are making some decisions that will change the enterprise. Flexibility, intellectual curiosity, and the drive to learn new things are essential in such an environment. A candidate can have everything else, but if they lack the growth gene they cannot help you.

Define the measurable accountability of each area/person hold to it

Group interview: The other team members must meet and assess each candidate. This accomplishes several things: First, it puts the team to work immediately. Seeking and providing such advice to you is the reason you formed an inner team in the first place. Second, the team knows what it needs and wants in a co-worker probably better than you do. They know where they lack expertise and where they already have it, avoiding needless duplication. They provide an independent review of each candidate. Use them and take their advice.

Use the 80% rule: If a candidate has 80% of what you need, then you must not disqualify them. This is a pretty good percentage. You can safely exclude those candidates who fall below this benchmark. However, those with at least 80% of the qualifications deserve a second and maybe third look.

Expectations that create a successful team

Think of an airliner filled with passengers. There are the right passengers and the wrong passengers. Throw off the wrong passengers. Now you're left with those who share a common *Why* and can move the enterprise toward accomplishing its mission.

Once you've assembled the very best team you can, it is time to manage their contribution. First, establish clear expectations for the team as a whole. They should participate in identifying these expectations. Quantify the results you're looking for—again, get the team to participate in defining and measuring the expected results. This gives the team a benchmark against which it can measure progress. Additionally, this holds the entire team accountable. That's the spirit of a team: They live and die together as one. Now there is no question as to their specific mission and the exact results they are accountable for achieving.

Provide a periodic feedback loop so the team can assess its actual progress against the expectations that it participated in creating. Make the feedback loop frequent enough—preferably on demand—so that the team can make immediate mid-course corrections to avoid missing targets they would have met had they just known there was a problem. This eliminates the excuse of poor intelligence as a reason for failure.

Reshuffling the deck

Notice that we refer to the team as an entity and as *it*. As far as the CEO is concerned, there are no individuals in the team. The team works for the CEO. The individuals who comprise the teamwork for the team. The team will manage its own members and will give each member their individual assignments and hold each accountable for their own success. If a team member is not performing, the team will help that individual improve. If necessary, the team will remove the individual and replace them with someone more qualified.

Hiring and firing a team member is a delicate and possibly litigious matter. The CEO should certainly guide the team in this process. But how do you and the team know when it's time to make a change? Here are some of the things you should look for when comparing your advisory team's capabilities against your vision for the enterprise:

- The current team or a member cannot take the company to the next level
- There is no appetite for new knowledge
- The members are not self starters
- They require a constant stream of stimulus to stretch their abilities
- They demonstrate little interest in how to get to the next rung of the ladder

- Many enterprises value their people in much the same way:
- Rainmakers at the top
- Support people and everyone else below

Certainly, money talks. That's why the rainmakers are so highly regarded throughout America's profit-oriented business climate. This is especially true in the professional firms—the law firms and public accounting firms. Don't know briefs from jockeys or a debit from a credit? No problem. Just so your license is current, if you control the big clients and bring in new money, you can write your own ticket.

However, rainmakers wouldn't get very far if they lacked the support of the mechanics and engineers who keep the ship running and on course. Of course, some of these back office specialists are rising stars in their own right. However, some are very happy right where they are. Upward mobility no longer holds any attraction for them. There is nothing wrong with this. Some of the happiest employees are those satisfied with their current jobs. They are experienced and do their jobs well.

Women in the workforce are often in this category. For example, say a law firm has a promising female associate who is doing a great job and has been identified as a potential partner. She, however, is starting a family and has no desire to put in the added hours and headaches that go with partnership no matter how much money she's leaving on the table. For many professional firms, the fast track is the only track. Up or out is a way of life that is understood from the first day of employment. However, in the case of this promising associate, the firm would be losing one of its best and brightest lawyers because her priorities were not the firm's.

The silent conversation

Imagine the stress both the law firm and this promising associate are undergoing. Both know that she has no desire to join the partnership. Both also know that she's going to be fired shortly because of it. What do you do as CEO?

You have the ability to step in and change things. Instead of keeping the silent conversation silent, give it voice and put it out there for everyone to see. You could create a secondary career path for those valued employees who don't want to become partners.

Professional firms that do this eliminate much of the stress on both the firm and its talented employees with different priorities in life. They are no less valuable to the firm because of it.

Retired on the job

This issue is a little more difficult to deal with if you're the CEO. There are long-standing employees who have put in a long and successful career at their company. They are looking at retiring in a year or two. They are just marking time until that day arrives. They take no initiative. They avoid putting forth anything more than the minimum effort required to keep their job.

Such employees are a blight on the workforce. They run down morale on those with a more proactive attitude. As CEO, how do you re-energize them? Failing that, how do you replace them?

Such long-standing employees have a vested interest in the company. You can't just fire them—their labor lawyer would take you to the cleaners. Giving them a meaningless job not only would depress everyone, it would waste a potentially valuable resource and could be construed as constructive termination. What do you do?

One answer is to suggest early retirement. They would not (nor should they) receive their full retirement benefits. Still, they would get what they want—out of the company—and you would free up a much needed space on the roster.

Alternatively, you could seek their counsel. Some of these about-to-retire employees have more experience than anyone. They know where the bodies are buried. Given a chance, they can be salvaged and placed in a position where they can use this knowledge for everyone's benefit. Some see themselves as antiquated war horses whose opinion no longer matters. These are the ones who desperately seek the respect they once had. Give them that and you'll likely see them pick up the traces and pull harder than ever. After all, you sought their opinion and gave them back their self-respect. You did them a huge favor and they won't forget it.

Tapping the Who, an example

Let's say that you're CEO of a manufacturing company that is ready to expand into a new set of products. To accomplish that, you need capital, engineering and manufacturing expertise in the new area. What do you do?

CEO's asking what to do are already out of their comfort zone. There's nothing wrong with that. No one knows everything. What is wrong is letting an opportunity pass you by just because you lack the background or resources to exploit it. Here are the steps the boss should take to gain access to those who can help.

Describe the expertise needed

In as much detail as possible, identify exactly what background, contacts and resources those who can help should bring to the table. For example, for the needed capital the CEO probably requires someone with:

- Experience and background in raising expansion capital
- Contacts with capital sources, private equity, venture capital and banking. These sources have a particular affinity for this type of deal in this industry and possess a strategic benefit to the company for their involvement.
- The ability to create a deal book describing the project and forecasting its likely financial performance to prospective lenders and investors
- The ability to structure the deal that makes sense for the company as well as the investors
- Experience in presenting the deal to likely investors
- A commitment to the CEO's purpose, cause and *Why* (such people also have the ability to obtain buy-in from the audience they're pitching).

This CEO is no longer flying blind in terms of the expertise required. This short list of attributes for the advisor who is raising the needed capital is not uncommon. These traits are found in most investment bankers and financial intermediaries working in the manufacturing sector.

Now all the CEO has to do is find several candidates, evaluate them according to the steps we've identified in this chapter and invite them to join in this extraordinary opportunity. This is not rocket science. There is nothing hard about it. What is hard, is trying to do the job without knowing what advice you need and how to get it.

Chapter 7 takes the *Why* and the *Who*, puts them together and makes them into a reality.

* * *

Chapter 7: Implementing: Making Your WHY Come Alive

The Navy SEAL motto is *The Only Easy Day Was Yesterday*. That's also true for guiding yourself and your enterprise to fulfilling your cause, purpose and *Why*. Figuring out the cause, surrounding yourself with those who share that purpose, developing the skill to hold a high stakes conversation, and remaining positive in the face of disaster are all easy compared to actually implementing the plan. But—and this is huge—putting together all of the previous pieces builds a foundation that makes the implementation of your plan possible. This chapter shows you how to implement the plan to fulfill your cause, purpose and *Why*.

Identifying the culture currently in place

They say that you must work with what you have. But first, you need to take an inventory of what's there to work with. Before implementing the plan, you need to determine just where the enterprise is currently. This essential first step tells you how receptive the key players will be to making the changes that a new plan necessitates.

Among the key members of the executive team, there must be a feeling of trust. That is, trust with one another, trust that everyone shares the same mission and trust that each has committed to the same cause, purpose and *Why*. This sense of trust creates a safe environment.

This sense of safety filters out to the team's willingness to take chances that could fail. They each need to know that their careers will not end if they try something promising and fail. They also must understand that there is no agenda other than the agenda everyone knows about.

The sense of safety gives the team a singular commonality. Only when its members feel confident around one another will a team gel into an effective unit. The culture of teamwork replaces the quest for individual stardom. Team members succeed as a unit, not as individuals. That is what the SEALs call *force projection*—the power of the team exceeds far beyond what is expected.

Interviewing team members

If you want to know a management team's current culture, just ask. However, there's definitely a right way to go about asking so that you obtain the information you need to make an informed judgment. You might start with some of these questions:

What's going well here? This helps you avoid trying to fix what isn't broken. It gives you a sense of what your people *think* works.

If you were in charge, what would you do differently? The troops usually have a different idea than do the generals. Of course they do. They're in the trenches. They get to see the effects of the decisions made by those merely observing from a distance. Some go about executing orders they know will fail. The idea is to give the executive making such ill-informed decisions enough rope so he'll eventually hang himself. A better idea would be to ask those implementing a decision what changes they would make to ensure its success. Asking this question let's those responsible for implementing the plan know what the entity should be doing differently.

What does the best culture look like for this entity? What works for one type of organization may not be best for another. An autocratic hierarchy such as a police department leads from the top down. Orders are issued and are expected to be followed. A think tank, on the other hand, would flounder under such a rigid culture as no new ideas or publishable understanding would ever likely surface.

Remember our example of Zappos, Tony Hsieh's online shoe store. Zappos' culture was one of hyper customer service. They live and breathe their customer's exquisite experience when shopping on Zappos. Hsieh created a recipe for fostering this culture at the company. There is no question that the culture Hsieh created at Zappos works extremely well to further the cause, purpose and *Why*. Would another culture work as well? Maybe. But why mess with success?

Don't limit the interviews to just the CEO and his toadies. Too often, those at the very top of an organization are too far removed to see the consequences of their actions. Further, they may have created a culture of fear that punishes employees for telling the higher-ups anything they don't wish to know. Consequently, if you limit your interviews to just the top people, you may get answers skewed in the direction of what they *want* to know rather than the truth. Get out among the employees and find out what's really going on in the enterprise's culture.

What is the company's real Why? This is another benchmarking question. Before your interviews begin, you may or may not know what your *Why* is. As CEO, you either clearly understand your cause and purpose or are compelled to discover it. The real question is if your inner team members share that identical commitment. That's why it often pays to have an independent third party doing the interviews. If the CEO does it herself, the answers may simply be mirroring back what they think she wants to hear.

Recall the earlier example of Sam Langley and his foray into manned flight. If you had asked him what his purpose was, he would have said to get humankind airborne. However, if you asked those on his team what the real purpose of the organization was, the answer would have likely been an honest, *To make Mr. Langley rich and famous by being first to fly.* Every decision Langley made was for the express purpose of promoting Langley.

What is your Why and how does it align with the company's?
You need to have an entire team committed to the same cause, purpose and *Why*. If you don't, then you'll never achieve the full measure of success. How do you know if the whole team shares this commitment? Ask them. If the culture is safe and there really are no repercussions for being honest, they will tell you.

What questions would you like to answer but were not asked?
This is perhaps the most important part of any interview. It gives everyone the chance to voice what's on their mind. Further, as the interviewer, you really don't know what you don't know. The answers you'll get will be illuminating.

Diagnosing the team's dynamics

Creating a team that will work together toward a common purpose first requires assessment of its functionality. To do this, you'll need to determine the team's internal dynamics. That is, see who leads, who follows, who says things just to please and who is not on board with your program.

Team dysfunctions usually come in five flavors. We identify them with a short survey. With that information, we can begin removing the dysfunctions that impede the team one by one. These five dysfunctions are:

- Lack of team cohesiveness and commitment
- Absence of trust
- Fear of conflict
- Accountability avoidance
- Disregard for results
- Lack of team cohesiveness

Effective teams work together. There are no individuals with different agendas. Everyone shares the same cause, purpose and *Why*. This must be especially true for your inner team. Additionally, the individual operating heads must understand that they're actually members of the executive team, with specialized departmental responsibilities. They are not warlords who own little fiefdoms.

Take America's law enforcement and counter terrorism efforts before the September 11, 2001 tragedy as an example. Before 911, the CIA didn't talk with the FBI and the New York City Fire Department wasn't even on the same communications frequencies as the police department. The reasons stem from interdepartmental rivalries largely caused by competition for budget dollars. As a result, response to these atrocities was uncoordinated and exceedingly slow.

That culture of independent, protected fiefdoms has been replaced with a more robust understanding of interdepartmental cooperation. We've made progress, but to the insiders there is still much dysfunctionality that needs correcting. An example is in the military—from the Joint Chiefs of Staff down to the foot soldiers, there is a fierce allegiance to their particular branch of service. The generals call this, *esprit de corps* and they encourage it. You can even hear it in the Navy SEAL's run to cadence songs they sing while training: ...*I don't wanna be no Recon...*
They're referring to the Marine Corp Force Reconnaissance, one of the most elite fighting forces on the face of the earth.

Absence of trust

Trust issues do not just stem from competition for scarce resources. People's personal agendas enter here. Your inner team members must trust each other's motives. They are there for a common purpose. If there's something else driving one or more member's actions, you will have an ineffective, dysfunctional team.

The absence of trust creates turf wars. It is polarizing. People will tend to choose sides. This is definitely disruptive to achieving the overall cause and purpose.

Fear of conflict

There will be conflict inside every team. Conflict is healthy. It challenges strategies and potential solutions. It creates new ones. However, the atmosphere must be safe for *productive* conflict (dissention) to thrive. It requires an honest, open team environment and culture.

A healthy team environment effectively uses conflict to move forward. It removes hostilities. It keeps the discussion objective with no chance of later retaliation just because someone disagrees.

Accountability avoidance

Team members must hold one another accountable for performing up to the level necessary for the team to accomplish its mission. This requires team members to challenge one another when they're not performing up to expectations. However, such challenge should not be adversarial. Instead, it must be given and accepted as helpful. Teams that hold their members accountable make better, faster decisions. There is never any question that those responsible for executing will achieve the results required. That means a high level of confidence by the team members in one another. Such confidence creates the CEO's confidence in the team's ability to achieve its purpose.

Inattention to results

Teams that are not properly attentive to the results they achieve often have no performance feedback mechanism. They need such a tool to measure their progress toward achieving required results.

The best feedback is provided either in real time or shortly thereafter. There must be time to make corrections in order to achieve projected results.

Taking it off site

There's a lot to be said for taking your inner team to an offsite location for their most vital discussions. It promotes uninterrupted dialog. Everyone is focused on the issues on *that* table and not on any other.

When you assemble your inner team to establish the cause, purpose and *Why,* you're sending a compelling message: This is really important and the team is the entity that's going to achieve the cause.

There are three steps to such an offsite team meeting: The first is to prioritize the issues. There may be a number of things you want to clear up that resulted from the questions and surveys conducted to get you to this point. For example, you might have discovered a lack of trust among two or more members of your team, or a team environment that doesn't promote a healthy type of constructive conflict among members. Whatever the issues, get them on the table.

With prioritization out of the way, it is the team's responsibility to resolve these issues. As CEO, you may be the team leader. Alternatively, the team may have someone else as its leader who reports to you. Whatever your role, now is the time to act as a facilitator. Let the team do its job in resolving these internal issues.

Lastly, devise an action plan for the team to fulfill its responsibility in achieving the common cause, purpose and *Why*. The plan must be specific and detailed. For example, it probably should contain a timeline with progress milestones. It should identify those responsible for specific tasks. It should also define the expected results quantitatively, if possible. This makes it easier to track progress against the feedback loop you've already created.

Managing the team's dynamics

Making the team function as a unit is not necessarily intuitive. Assessing and managing team dynamics is a discipline unto itself. However, there are some techniques you can use to ensure the team's progress doesn't stop just because its dynamics in working together hit a speed bump.

First is confidentiality. The team members must feel totally free to voice their opinions honestly, knowing what they say will not be repeated outside the team. This confidential structure insulates the team. They can feel free to try out new ideas and theories, no matter how odd they may at first appear. After all, no one but the trusted team members will ever hear of such an idea that remained on the drawing board with good reason.

Focus the team on the overarching mission it confronts. The smaller decisions that get us there are not so important at this stage. For example, let's say that the CEO's inner team at a manufacturing company is looking at a bleak future. It has concluded that its products are now commodities that everyone makes. This situation has squeezed profit margins to the point where it no longer makes financial sense for the company to manufacture these products. What to do?

A CEO's Secret Weapon

That's the issue confronting this team. The team's deliberations and its conclusions will affect the company and its employees forever more. The team evaluated a number of alternatives. At the end, it concluded the most sustainable strategy was to transform the company's business model.

The team's short, clear statement of purpose became: "Within 2 years, transform operations from manufacturing to distribution and logistics." With this mission clear, the next step was to identify what they were getting themselves into with such a sea change. To figure this out, the team began asking questions of the person on the team who was leading this initiative.

Rules of engagement for the focus person

The person leading a particular initiative—the focus person—accepts responsibility for defending her idea. This is not an adversarial inquisition. It is a process to identify the issues surrounding such a strategic change in the business as that being proposed. The focus person *has the right not to answer a question.* Questions that go unanswered by their nature may reveal far more than any answer a team member might provide. What makes these questions so important? Fresh questions lead to fresh actions and therefore better results.

Another rule of engagement for the focus person to enforce is that all questions must help the issue rather than simply satisfy the questioner's curiosity. There should be no statements of history like, "I heard of one company that did this back in '02…" That's not a question.

Further, there is no grilling or cross-examining. An example of a question that helps push the issue forward is one where the questioner could not possibly know the answer. For example,

"Did you ever see a manufacturer switch to distribution and logistics before?"

Additionally, silence is okay. There are frequent lulls in question/answer sessions. It simply means people are processing information and gaining new insights. Eventually, all the questions and answers about the new initiative will be on the table. At this point, the team knows what else it needs to know to determine if this is the most viable solution to the company's predicament and how to begin implementation.

Making decisions

From this process comes the information required to begin making some decisions related to implementation of the strategic initiative. There are some ways to help facilitate this process.

Decision making in groups of any size is a question of group dynamics. There is always someone who is the Alpha. This person may be helpful to the overall process or she may be totally out to lunch. Regardless, if you are the group leader, you should not allow the Alpha to gain control over the group.

Controlling the Alpha

There's a technique to keep the Alpha in the group from taking over and moving the agenda off point. It's called PrOACT. This stands for:

Problem: Be sure the team stays focused on the right issue—not the issue the Alpha wants
Objective: Specify the objective and keep reminding the team why they're there and what they need to accomplish
Alternatives: Create imaginative alternatives when the team gets stuck

Consequences: Make sure everyone involved understands the consequences of not making a decision and/or making the wrong decision.

Trade-off: Decisions are rarely all good or all bad. There will be some trade-offs with each choice. Identify them. Quantify them in terms of financial impact, and the other metrics critical to measuring the enterprise's performance.

Using the PrOACT framework for the decision making process can help keep your team on track.

As team leader, you can also use these four techniques for controlling the group dynamics at work:

Focus on what's important. This can be difficult if the Alpha keeps trying to draw the conversation off point and toward their agenda. Nevertheless, don't allow them to do it.

Maintain logic and consistency. The faster a group moves the more errors it makes. Their logic patterns may stray. You'll see inconsistencies arise. When that happens, stop the conversation and slow things down. Go back, correct any errors, and put the conversation back on track.

Relevant information. Encourage and guide the gathering of relevant information. This ensures that the team has all the information it requires to make informed decisions.

Too much information. The discussion leader is responsible for extracting only as much information and analysis as is necessary to resolve a particular dilemma. Information provided beyond that—no matter how relevant—wastes everyone's time because it won't be used. Don't allow the team to commit the cardinal sin of analysis paralysis just to avoid making the hard choices.

Visualizing potential solutions

Once you think the team has come up with the most viable solution(s) there are some things you can do to determine what it might look like if implemented. Visualizing how a particular decision might affect the rest of the company isn't difficult. However, it does require making some assumptions on behavior.

The easiest way to visualize a decision working is to create a financial model of how the company would react. Usually, these begin with the enterprise's financial statements put into a computer model. Then insert the assumptions that drive the revenues, expenses, assets and liabilities that the subject decision will affect. Run the model over a number of possible success and failure ranges. We're looking for the *range* of profitability and cash flow the company will see if the idea is very successful or an abject failure.

Once you have that range, you've identified your tolerable error. That is, the potential cost you're willing to pay (from failure) in exchange for a chance to hit a homerun (the top of the success range). The next question is how to lessen the potential risk of loss without affecting the upside too much.

Implementation planning

By now, the CEO's team knows the answers to the questions posed during the focus person's time in the hot seat. These answers will form the basis of the implementation plan. Out of this process comes:

- The important initiatives that drive this decision
- The ideas for implementation and the priorities of each
- Specific decisions needed to move the implementation forward.

Generating buy-in effectively

★ NET Growth focus

A CEO's Secret Weapon

Implementing your cause, purpose and *Why* means gaining the team's understanding, commitment, and ultimately, their action supporting these goals. Gaining buy-in is the most valuable ability any leader has. If it was easy, anyone could do it. Few can. Buy-in requires influencing people's thoughts and feelings.

The strongest leaders are those who create a positive vision of the future. They paint a "big picture" that taps into people's emotions. Their vision for the future paints a picture that fulfills their audience's agenda and makes them say, "Yes! You understand me. Count me in." Finally, these persuasive leaders know how to ask for a commitment and inspire their listeners to take steps toward achieving the [now] common goal.

If this sounds manipulative, it is to some extent. Think of the televangelists. They employ the extreme outer edges of this same buy-in technique. By the time they are finished, the audience is reaching into their pockets and pulling out the checkbook.

Telling your story

The story of your cause, purpose and *Why* must mesh with people's agenda for them to buy in. There must be common ground between you and your audience. This common ground is your cause, purpose and *Why*. The secret to generating buy-in is to design and deliver a story that projects a *positive* future for your audience. Then, connect the dots between the future you want (your cause, purpose and *Why*) and the future your audience wants (their agenda). This link shows how buying into your cause is the fastest, surest way to fulfilling their agenda. If you listen to most politicians' stump speeches, this is exactly the technique they employ. It works.

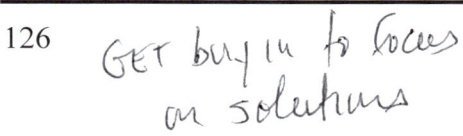

The most useful technique in constructing the story of your cause is to present things in three's. Begin by developing your story in three chapters. Make these the three most important ways this idea fulfills the audience's agenda. Often these three items focus on the audience's needs, wants and future goals. Then tie these to your cause, purpose and *Why*. Answer the question of how your purpose fulfills the audience's agenda. Cite three of the most important ways.

Cement this vital connection by providing three short examples of how it works, and then lead into your call to action. Tell the audience clearly and exactly what their next step must be in order to fulfill their agenda. Close by asking for a definite commitment from each participant right now.

Your 12-week plan

Most enterprises plan at least twelve months into the future. Some update that plan every six months to allow for making mid-course corrections. I think even six months is too long to wait before evaluating progress and making the necessary changes. No plan survives contact with the enemy. For business, there are so many enemies—competition, regulation, legislation, the list goes on. Waiting to adjust your plan for even six months could put you out of business. Instead, create two planning horizons: The strategic horizon can be one year out. That serves as a long-term guide for the three-month tactical plans to reach. Each three-month plan must be actionable and reasonable. By the time the fourth quarterly plan is accomplished, you have achieved your one-year strategic goals.

Who should make this all happen?

It would be nice if the CEO had the skills required to do all the things necessary to make their cause, purpose and *Why* come true. However, that's not typically the case. The CEO would have to be a rare renaissance man to have all the skills and background needed to run the company *and* to implement the things needed to make their purpose a reality.

So who should undertake responsibility for achieving the *Why*? This highly skilled individual must have a deep knowledge and background in using the tools that effectively guide people toward the desired result. Usually, these individuals come from outside the enterprise. Some are hired as high-level employees, to serve the CEO. Others are kept as independent consultants. Except for the duration of their involvement, it really doesn't matter how they're brought aboard. Just so they are there and have the authority needed to do their work.

Some CEO's balk at the cost of this undertaking. After all, if the CEO can't make her *Why* come true, then it's going to take a very skilled person to do it for her. These people don't come without a cost. However, the real cost is failing to achieve the cause, purpose and *Why*. Where a truly professional and skilled facilitator may be paid in money, the opportunity cost for not engaging her services will ultimately be many times whatever her professional fees are.

Chapter 8, "The Power of Being Fully Engaged", brings us back to the CEO's challenge of remaining involved in all the details that make the enterprise successful.

* * *

Chapter 8: Growing the enterprise

Every CEO wishing to grow their enterprise, expand their cause, purpose and *Why* and become more profitable, goes through many of the same stages of evolution. Each presents its own challenges. Additionally, there's a sequence to every growth pattern. My research from interviewing many, many CEOs uncovered eight stages of growth:

- Research
- Pre-revenue
- Infancy—zero to $1 million in revenue
- Profitability
- Positive cash flow
- Crossing the chasm
- Adolescence
- Adulthood

Here's how each relates to growing the enterprise.

Research

Most enterprises begin with an idea. Ideas require research to prove their validity. For engineering and other technical areas, the research can take significant amounts of time and be hugely expensive. Take for example, a company called AngelMed Systems (www.angel-med.com). This medical device start-up has been researching and proving its idea for a cardiac monitoring device for ten years now. It has cost north of $50 million in investor's money getting to the final FDA trials.

AngelMed's CEO, David Fischell, has a cause, purpose and *Why* that is persuasive—save the lives of the million plus people around the world every year who would have otherwise died of a heart attack. With AngelMed's Guardian system, these cardiac patients receive advanced warning of a cardiac event with enough time to get to a hospital and receive treatment **before** the heart attack ever occurs. Already, during its clinical trials around the world, Guardian has saved the lives of hundreds.

Investors share CEO Fischell's cause, purpose and *Why*. As a result, AngelMed has reached the final stages before receiving FDA approval. It has been a long and expensive road. The anticipated results and benefits to cardiac patients around the world will be worth the struggle.

For other types of enterprises—those without regulatory overseers—the research is often confined to proving there is a market for the product. These CEOs know how to build their product. All they need is someone to buy it.

Such enterprises are too often a nifty solution in search of a problem to solve. We find this especially in engineering companies producing consumer devices. The principals are often brilliant engineers. They have a passion for solving puzzles. And they do a great job. However, too often the technology and devices they create have too small a demand in the market place to make it economically viable.

Certainly, the principals are disappointed when the research reveals there's really no point in continuing with the product. However, it is much better to find this out before investing the precious time and investor dollars in a project that will ultimately fail to gain traction in the marketplace.

Pre-revenue

Let's assume the research tells us the enterprise has a fighting chance of survival. From this we have at least some confidence the cause, purpose and *Why* can be fulfilled. So we raise investment capital and start the company.

A CEO's Secret Weapon

We establish our production facilities. We hire the accountants who will tell us how profitable we are. But wait. The accountants do not yet have revenue to put against costs and compute profits.

The pre-revenue stage is just that. The CEO is just getting the company underway. The production facilities aren't up and running yet. Suppliers are skeptical when dealing with a start-up. They want to see some hard money before shipping the raw materials.

This is the scariest time of a start-up's life. There's no cash coming into the company and lots going out. As a result, the CEO is often doing some very un-CEO-like jobs. So is everyone else. They are trying to limit the burn rate of investment capital. The accountants all too often present cash flow reports that compute mere days of cash left.

Still, the CEO believes in her cause, purpose and *Why*. Pre-revenue just means that the money inflow hasn't yet begun. At this stage, the CEO hasn't yet figured out how to turn on the money flow.

Mark Coker is the CEO of Smashwords, the e-Book publishing company. Mark just knew that what he had created was a disruptive technology in the publishing industry—allowing authors themselves to self-publish their e-Books. The Smashwords platform was easy to use, fast and allowed the author to set the book price. It turned publishing's economic model upside down—giving the authors the majority of the revenue generated from book sales.

The problem was, in the early days, Smashwords had few authors publishing few e-books and selling to even fewer readers. Gross revenue for one early stage month was less than $10.

That is until CEO Coker discovered the valve that opened the revenue pipeline. He arranged for the publishing industry's biggest outlets to take Smashwords books and sell them on their own platforms. Suddenly Smashwords authors were being sold on Amazon, Apple's iTunes, Kobo, Diesel, Barnes and Noble and Baker-Taylor. Smashwords survived and went from the pre-revenue stage to the infancy stage in just a few short months.

Infancy—zero to $1 million in revenue

During their infancy stage, most companies aren't making much in revenue. The CEO's challenge is to maintain the momentum that just recently got the company airborne while installing the systems that will control it. These are the marketing systems, finance and accounting systems, systems of internal accounting controls, and human resources policies and procedures.

At first, none of these will be robust. They don't need to be. However, they must provide some reporting of key performance metrics in timely feedback to the CEO. All sorts of problems will arise during this stage. Everything is new and there are no tried and true fixes when things go wrong. The company is inventing solutions as they go.

The CEO doesn't know yet what he's doing. Yes, the company has created the first revenue. Still, the challenge is three-fold:

- Keep the revenue stream sustainable and regular
- Convert that initial revenue stream to profits
- Convert those profits into cash flow

Everyone at an infancy stage company is selling—or at least they should be. Maintaining the current revenue and increasing it is the first priority. The CEO must achieve a critical mass of repeat customers to sustain the company and move it into the next stage—profitability.

Right behind selling in the order of priority is getting the operations going. This includes the systems and the people that actually make the enterprise function. All this and without losing sight of your cause, purpose and *Why*. *And*, at the same time, doing all those little things to achieve the overall purpose.

One danger here is allowing the CEO and other founders to revert back to what they do best, rather than what the company needs them to do. For example, a brilliant programmer may have founded a software development company. That is what she's best at and it is what she loves doing. Fine. Great. But once the product programming is complete and the first revenues begin dribbling in, the programmer/CEO cannot continue programming. She must switch gears.

The CEO becomes the chief salesperson. She also is the head motivator and establishes the corporate culture necessary to fulfill the cause. Her love of programming becomes a distant memory. First on her list of things to do is establish a sustainable revenue stream.

Profitability

Think of the pre-profitability stage as the company's infancy. Sales exist, though, they're small—probably $1 million to $10 million. Remember, profit does not necessarily equate to cash flow. For some capital-intensive industries, cash flow can still greatly lag profits or even be negative.

Still, in this infancy stage, the company is earning a steady stream of profits. Its products exist and are proven in the market place. Now is the time to begin hiring the professionals and forming the internal organizations that will take the company to the next level. These are the finance and accounting, marketing, engineering and operations departments.

A CEO's Secret Weapon

The CEO can no longer oversee everything himself. It is these professionals who assume responsibility for their departments. They also become the CEO's direct reports. They are accountable for achieving planned results. These people will design the products, make the products, push the products out the door to the eagerly awaiting hands of your customers and then collect their money.

Sales at infancy and pre-profitability companies are usually $1 million to $10 million in revenue. Because virtually every cent made is being invested right back into the company, you are only breaking even or even losing money.

That's expected at this stage of development. The CEO's challenge is to create additional, more profitable products quickly. Your company cannot survive as a one-trick pony. Be an innovator. Take the technology and expertise that created your first product and immediately design and tool up for the next one and the one after that.

This is the time for the CEO to get out of the office—because there are direct reports to oversee daily operations—and go see customers and key suppliers. Listen to what they have to say. Understand their pain. Figure out how your company can make that pain go away with a new product or perhaps just an innovative change to one that already exists. Figure out what they're really buying when they buy your product.

For example, if you manufacture and sell drill presses, what's the customer really buying? Holes. Precisely cut holes of a specific size down to the micrometer. Holes placed in exact places. Make no mistake; they're not buying your drill press. They're buying what it does.

An enterprising CEO might take that knowledge and make a call on the sheet metal fabricator who sells to raw materials buyers. The pitch would go something like this:

"You sell sheet metal, tons of sheet metal. Your buyers have to take that sheet metal—that they can get anywhere—and cut holes in it using my drill presses. How about you lease a few of my drill presses so you can cut the holes in your sheet metal for your customers? You've just added huge value and savings for your customers. You've also just differentiated yourself from every one of your competitors. Your profit margins just soared and you eliminated much of your competition."

This CEO just opened up a new market for his drill presses. Certainly, not every customer will buy pre-drilled sheet metal. But many will. This kind of innovative thinking goes a long way to moving out of the pre-profitability stage and into the profit and positive cash flow stage.

The challenge every CEO faces is coming up with a constant stream of new and potentially tipping-point ideas. At first, the CEO and some key people will do the R&D. However, shortly, they will establish a professional R&D department and hire those who can do a better job.

Positive cash flow

After you've steered your company from the red and into the black, there's yet another hurdle you must conquer. Generating positive cash flow often lags profitability. There are always irritating little nuisances like customers stretching their payables—of which yours are one. Then there are your vendors who, despite your best efforts, naturally want to be paid sooner than later.

135

These and a host of other cash guzzlers conspire to eat away at this most precious of assets. Nevertheless, generating positive cash flow is essential for any enterprise to sustain itself.

Positive cash flow provides CEOs a margin of error. This comes in the form of an increasing bank balance of excess, unallocated cash. Should something go wrong—like a new product failing to take off as anticipated—the company can live to fight another day.

Investors especially like to see positive cash flow. To them it means a smaller cash call, or no cash call, in the future. The downside is that they see the increasing bank balance as belonging to them. Soon questions will arise as to just when the board will declare a cash dividend for these faithful and patient investors.

In spite of these issues, positive cash flow signals that the enterprise is self-sustaining. From this point, the CEO is ready to cross the chasm from an R&D and technology development shop to a real marketing enterprise.

Crossing the chasm

This is a term born of the tech boom. It marks the time when a company successfully makes the transition from customers who are enthusiasts and early adopters (of which there are few) to mass-market customers (of which there are many). Soon your customer base, market segments served, and the uses for your products begin growing—geometrically, if you're lucky. That's what the venture capitalists calls *scalability*. You must have it or prove that you will have it before the top tier venture funds will show an interest in your company. Here's what the chasm looks like:

Crossing the Chasm

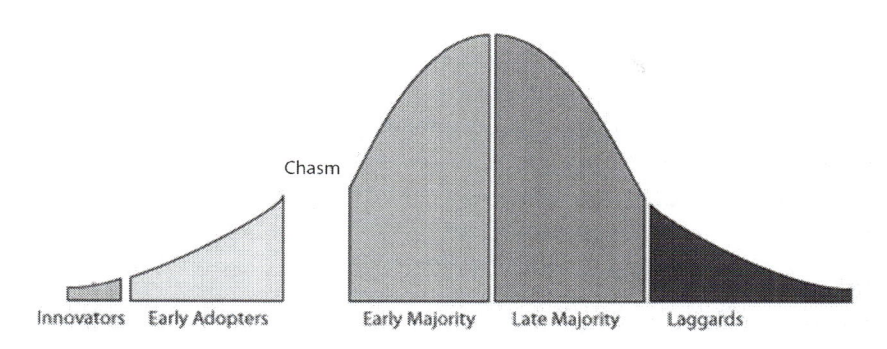

[Chart showing adoption curve with categories: Innovators, Early Adopters, Chasm, Early Majority, Late Majority, Laggards]

There's a big gap between the early adopters and the beginnings of true marketing scale.

The iPod is a spectacular example of a technology-intense product that crossed the chasm into the mainstream marketplace and became a cultural phenomenon. At first only the true Apple fans bought the iPod. Then Apple's marvelously successful marketing machine took over. They sold the iPod as a beautiful product that appeals to a passionate group of users as well as everyone else. Join us, urged Apple. The iPod soon became a statement about its owner—savvy, capable, willing to leave the main stream and march to their own tune (played on their iPods, of course). They were hip and fashionable.

As the iPod aged, it got better, simpler and grew in its capabilities. Then the iPod owners did something not even Apple's marketing team could do. The iPod's fans took it viral. They loved their little devices. And they couldn't wait to tell anyone willing to listen about it. The owners became iPod evangelists. Suddenly, the iPod became the ubiquitous gold standard of its product class.

Once you've crossed the chasm into scalability, you've probably achieved consistent profitability and a reliable, positive cash flow. Next, come the problems associated with such success.

Adolescence—$10 million to $50 million in revenue

This stage of development confounds so many CEOs. They're finally sustainable. With annual revenues between $10-$50 million they are no longer a tiny business. However, many such companies still cling to that small business mentality. Their systems are strained because the CEO has failed to build the team that can sustain such increased activity. Customers begin to notice, deliveries lag beyond the dates promised, and Human Resources cannot keep pace with the demand for employees with the specific skills needed. Too often, the CEO herself is still trying to do things the way she did when the company was in its infancy. When this happens, the CEO becomes the bottleneck to effective decision-making.

The adolescence stage is when the CEO needs to take her hands off of direct control of the wheel and hand it over to her team. The team reports to the CEO. They are responsible for direct day-to-day operations. That's how to turn the chaos of adolescence into order.

Developing the brand

During the adolescence period the company is still finding its way. It has tried a number of things; some didn't work, but many did. Those solutions that worked produced far more success than the cost of failures. The company is developing an identity all its own.

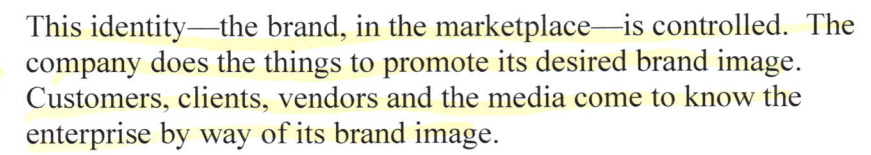

This identity—the brand, in the marketplace—is controlled. The company does the things to promote its desired brand image. Customers, clients, vendors and the media come to know the enterprise by way of its brand image.

The brand image should distinguish the company from the competition. Zappos, the Website selling shoes, has a brand

A CEO's Secret Weapon

image that emphasizes customer experience; they are truly passionate about serving their customers. They beefed up their customer care department and the training. Indeed, everyone at Zappos considers themselves to be customer care representatives. They are empowered to do anything it takes to please their customers. Further, they all speak with the same voice when it comes to customer service. It works.

Creating disruptive technologies thru innovation

During the adolescent stage, opportunities to best the competition sometimes arise. The most successful way to best the competition is to develop a disruptive technology—disruptive to the competition.

If disruptive technology thrives in small, nimble and emerging companies, then sustaining technology is the favorite of large, bureaucratic enterprises. Sustaining technology seeks merely incremental improvements to an already established and proven technology. Cost savings is often a byproduct of innovations in sustaining technology.

Disruptive technology, on the other hand, is new. It doesn't have the refinement of its sustainable brother. Maybe it doesn't yet have a proven, practical application. Alexander Graham Bell's "electrical speech machine," was such a disruptive technology. Now it is the telephone.

Disruptive technologies typically have low profit margins, but potentially explosive, immensely scalable demand. Because of the risk and the low margins, large, established enterprises often dismiss proposals for disruptive technologies.

IBM dismissed Bill Gates when he tried to sell them his brand new DOS operating system for use in a personal computer. This went directly against IBM's corporate mandate of just big-iron installations. They failed to see the potentially explosive demand for Gates' vision of how computers would be used by individuals every single day rather than just by large installations on a project basis. Gates smoked them with his disruptive technology.

Disruptive technologies are perfect for the more nimble, less risk adverse adolescent stage companies. Some of the best ideas now come from small, early stage companies with a culture that rewards innovation rather than stomping the life from it. The result is that disruptive technologies have a history of blindsiding their larger competitors. As the technology matures and gains a larger audience and market share, it threatens the status quo. This is just what an adolescent stage company should be doing.

Adulthood—$50 million in revenue and beyond

Being the boss is not easy. Each development stage presents its own challenges. Adulthood is no exception. If you thought the CEO could put it on cruise control at that this stage, better think again.

By the time an enterprise has $50 million or more in revenue, it is established in its market place. Distribution channels work. The various systems and controls that keep the company running every day are in place and work. The CEO has engineered a brand that resonates with customers and vendors.

However, many adulthood companies become victims of their own success. Unless you're careful, complacency can creep into the management team. This trickles down to every employee. Suddenly, the things that made the company successful—the cause, purpose and *Why*—get lost in the daily shuffle. Here's how it happens.

Phase 1: Everyone shares the cause

A CEO's Secret Weapon

Think back to what made the enterprise great. The biggest positive attribute was that everyone had a shared purpose. Every day was war and every person was fighting the same fight against a common enemy.

If the CEO had to list the attributes that made the enterprise successful they would probably include:

- Everyone was focused and directed toward the same goal
- There was high energy resulting from the number of wolves at the door
- There was a shared optimism that this would succeed
- Communication up and down the line was fast and accurate—largely because there wasn't much of a line for it to travel
- Since the team started from scratch there was a culture of continuous improvement with little downside if an idea didn't work
- There was passionate leadership focused on a clear cause, purpose and *Why* that was simple and clearly communicated.

Phase 2: Lost purpose

This loss of purpose can come at any time during the company's evolution. However, we most often see it during adulthood. The founders who made the company what it is today are disengaged from daily operations. Instead, they hired professional managers to run the company for them.

Many of the initial employees grew disenchanted and left—along with their passion for the cause. Those working for a paycheck rather than a shared *Why* replaced them. Eventually the original *Why* got so diluted that it is all but unrecognizable as anything but folklore from a bygone era.

A cynical, negative atmosphere creeps onto the shop floor. The blame game and declining productivity replaces teamwork and a passion for problem solving.

n example is a substantial grocery chain in Colorado. This company had grown from a single store to over 130 locations with 13,000 [unionized] employees. Then they forgot how they created such success. Their *Why* once included a passionate devotion to their customers. This was equaled by their attention to quality—a killer combination. There wasn't much of a bureaucracy so all employees got a lot of face time with the senior executives and owners.

Then with their rapid growth and unionization, they lost these vital cultural ingredients. The company began struggling. They stumbled over their cause, purpose and *Why*.

Phase 3: *Transforming and reinventing*

Smart management teams recognize the symptoms of an enterprise losing its purpose. They even understand the importance of reuniting with the *Why*. Few know how to get it done. They need to refresh the company and recapture the entrepreneurial spirit that once guided the company.

The first step of Phase 3 is to take stock and assess the current corporate culture. This self-analysis is intensely introspective. It focuses on rediscovering the cause, purpose and *Why*. During the process, everyone in the company will examine the core values—those that once were, those now present, and those the company needs to adopt. This forces the company as a whole to decide which of the cultural characteristics exhibited today to hold on to and which to discard. They must also decide which new cultural imperatives they must insert into the mix to reverse the downward plunge. Lastly, they need to determine what they need to do to move on.

These cultural reinforcements, changes and additions must involve everyone in the company. It cannot be limited to the executive suite. The Colorado grocery store chain I introduced back in Phase 2 did this. The results produced a sea change in the way everyone thought about the company and their role in it. The way they accomplished this change was also very smart.

Rather than appointing someone from within the company to oversee the diagnosis and transformation, they hired an outside expert who had done this many times before. There was instant trust in this individual. She could not possibly have any motive other than to improve the overall company. She did not belong to the union. As a result, she was respected and listened to. Her advice and counsel was accepted. Her instructions were followed. A successful transformation resulted.

Phase 4: Writing the next chapter

Until now, we've simply pulled back on the stick to stop the plane from continuing its death spiral. Yes, we now have level flight. But we're not done yet. We now have the opportunity to hit the throttles and begin the upward climb to the next level of success.

There are several things the CEO must weld into the enterprise. The first and most significant is creating a culture of training and learning. Every growth company needs fresh ideas from its people. Often the best ideas come from those with years of experience but whose ideas were never sought out. Training people how to apply their experience to contribute to a culture of continuous improvement pays huge dividends.

The next chapter in the enterprise's success story also comes from doing the research—both technology and market research. Determine not only what is possible, but also what will sell in the marketplace.

The creativity to dream up new products and market segments cannot be done alone. Small groups forming alliances that have complimentary skills will write the enterprise's next chapter. They will experiment with concepts and ideas until they have the makings for a potential new venture.

The Cycle of Renewal

Most enterprises and organizations go through these four phases. The CEO who learns how to guide the organization through the process is indeed a learned individual. However, even after successfully navigating through the process, the work is not complete (CEOs can never rest).

Over time, they'll have to initiate the same process again and again. Pressing the Refresh Button is a fact of corporate life. This is the single most compelling leadership attribute of the great CEO's. Yes, each is a good manager and an even better delegator. However, they are always watching for signs of complacency. If you are the CEO, your job is to ensure that everything is working properly.

CEOs are strategic thinkers and visionaries. Their role is not daily management. Their job is to keep things moving toward the fulfillment of the organization's strategic objectives, all the while communicating the *Why*.

* * *

Chapter 9: The Power of Why

Power is being aware of the action you've chosen, possessing the freedom to do it, and exercising that power intentionally. Power is the freedom to involve ourselves in meaningful activities. Power is our personal participation in creating our reality.

Every CEO is married to power. They work to get it; they work to maintain it. The best ones work to judiciously use it to accomplish their cause, purpose and *Why* (the CPW). There are six aspects of executive power that facilitate its attainment, use and maintenance:

- The power that goes with being fully engaged in your CPW
- The power of focus
- The power of resilience
- The power of habits
- The power that comes from staying out of your own way
- The power of learning from past mistakes—this is the power of *failing forward*

This chapter illuminates each of these six components of power and shows you how to use it to achieve your goals.

The Power of full engagement

For most, being fully engaged means they are present (mentally, physically and in any other way), involved, and active in achieving the CPW. Full engagement is the energy state that best achieves the targeted performance. Full engagement requires the expenditure of physical energy, achieving an emotional connection, becoming mentally focused on your goals and being spiritually aligned with a purpose that is greater than your immediate self-interests.

Energy management

Energy, not time, fuels high performance. Everything people do—from interacting with colleagues and making decisions to spending time with their families—requires energy. The results of any activity or assignment are reduced without the right quantity, quality, focus and force of energy.

The same holds true for organizations. Great leaders are first stewards of organizational energy. They mobilize, focus, invest, channel, renew and expand the energy of others. A CEO's job is to manage the organization's energy and focus it on the things that will achieve the cause, purpose and *Why*. They begin by effectively managing their own energy. This efficiency and focus of purpose becomes a role model for the rest of the organization. Four key energy management principles drive this process:

Principle 1: Energy sources

Organizations draw their energy from the people who work there. There are four separate but related sources of energy that each of us has:

- Physical
- Emotional
- Mental
- Spiritual

Evaluate the amount of physical energy in the qualitative terms of high, medium and low. This gives a useful index as to the amount. Similarly, measure emotional capacity in terms of its quality: positive, neutral or negative.

Mental energy is a little tougher to evaluate. Think in terms of alertness or original thought. Again, if you wan to quantify it, use imprecise high, medium and low gradients. Spiritual energy is something altogether different. Rather than a religious connotation, I use spiritual energy to describe the organization's or a person's faith and commitment to the cause, purpose and *Why*. Without sufficient spiritual energy, no one will succeed in moving the organization toward the CPW.

Principle 2: Balancing energy levels

The energy everyone brings to the cause is fragile. It decomposes and dwindles almost as soon as it begins. Overuse or—worse—underuse causes an enterprise's energy to decay even faster. Because energy is an asset with a limited half-life, we balance its expenditure with periodic energy recharges.

This is true for people as well as enterprises. Those with the richest, happiest and most productive lives possess the ability to fully engage in the challenge at hand. However, they can also disengage periodically and recharge their batteries.

Those who describe themselves as workaholics have an imbalance. This imbalance of energy actually makes them less productive over the long run than their well-balanced counterparts. Given a choice, I always hire the well-balanced CEO candidate rather than the one who describes herself as a happy workaholic. Experience teaches that such individuals lead less satisfying lives, leave a string of divorces, misguided and unguided children, and erratic performance in their wake.

The purpose of balancing energy levels is to have a sufficient energy supply available to accomplish the planned tasks with some left over for the emergencies that inevitably occur. After you've balanced energy levels, have scheduled periods of diminished activity so everyone can recharge in anticipation of the next ramp-up in activity.

A CEO's Secret Weapon

Over extended periods, the organization and everyone in it arrives at a manageable energy level that is sufficient to achieve the objectives without killing themselves in the process. It is sustainable.

Principle 3: Building capacity

Like any athlete, building capacity requires training beyond normal operating limits, then falling back to recharge. Organizations and the people in them build emotional, mental and spiritual capacity in the same way. Creating a capacity in each requires expending energy beyond ordinary limits and then recovering. In other words, you have to work at developing physical, mental, emotional and spiritual energy. Stress that creates fatigue expands capacity. The more stress, the more fatigue, but also the more endurance you're creating. You work hard—beyond what you would normally—then fall back to reenergize and recover.

Attempting to run at full speed all the time—as some law firms demand of their associates—creates more long-term problems than they solve. We call this entropy—the second law of thermodynamics. It states that energy flows spontaneously from regions of higher temperature to regions of lower temperature in the form of heat. The faster the process runs and for a longer period, the more heat is developed until entropy accumulates in the system. It gets even worse. The more heat developed, the higher the likelihood that something will break because of it. Eventually, the accumulated heat dissipates in the form of wasted energy. The system enters a state of disorder and chaos ensues.

As CEO, you want the enterprise to run at its optimum rate—high enough to accomplish the task and to make things challenging, but not so high as to burn up the mechanism. Be sure to insert periodic times for adequate recovery.

Principle 4: Positive energy rituals

Maintaining an energy level that is appropriate for the task is the key to full engagement and sustained high performance. Developing rituals to manage your energy level without thinking about it is one path to sustained performance. Building positive energy rituals requires defining precise behaviors and performing them at specific times. The intent is to manage your energy level without thinking about it.

A positive energy ritual is a behavior that becomes automatic over time. It is fueled by a deeply held value. Positive rituals insure that we use as little conscious energy as possible where it is not absolutely necessary. This energy management autopilot frees us to strategically focus on creative, enriching activities that further our cause, purpose and *Why*. Creating positive rituals is the most powerful means to manage energy when fully engaged.

Concurrent with creating positive energy rituals is the change that goes with them. Creating lasting change is a three-step process:

Define Purpose: Identify and describe your most important values both personally and professionally. These deep values and the vision that accompanies them fuel a high-octane source of energy for change. It also serves as a compass for navigating through and around the storms that inevitably come between you and your goals.

Face the Truth: Creating change requires an honest look at who you are today. The first question is, *How are you spending your energy?* Facing the truth begins with gathering credible data.

Take Action: Close the gap between who you are and who you want to be. Along with that, identify how you manage your energy now and what changes you must make to achieve your goals. Taking action requires a personal development plan grounded in positive energy rituals.

A CEO's Secret Weapon

What do I do best?

The Power of Focus

Directing your focus to the right tasks and projects is among the most important skills a leader can develop. The best leaders invest the vast majority of their time doing what they do best and delegate the other tasks to those who are better at them than they are. Certainly, they hold those to whom they have delegated responsibilities accountable for the results. However, with effective controls and periodic progress updates, the leader develops a confidence that these delegated tasks are tracking the way they should.

Looking for what you do best

The greatest results come from focusing your time and energy on doing the things at which you are truly brilliant. So ask yourself:

- What do I do effortlessly and without much study, thought or preparation?
- What do I do easily that others find difficult?
- What opportunities exist in today's marketplace for the areas where I excel?

Focusing on what you do best and moving such projects to the top of your priority list works. Make this reorganization of your priorities part of your daily work plan. You'll see dramatic jumps in productivity, results and probably your income.

There's a cute description of how to identify your top priorities for each day. It's the 4-D Solution:

- Dump it
- Delegate it
- Defer it
- Do it

150

A CEO's Secret Weapon

For example, think of how you review your list of incoming emails each morning. What thought process do you use to decide the disposition of each? Chances are it's similar to the 4-D Solution. Most emails you simply delete as unimportant to achieving your priorities. The next level is usually those emails that should not have come to you in the first place. Chances are someone who just wanted the boss to know they were working sent them to you. Delegate those to the appropriate person. Then have a word with the sender as to why they are wasting your time.

Those emails that have survived the first two cuts have some interest. However, your time is valuable. Many you can defer dealing with them until they come up in your priority list. The remaining emails are those that you know you need to read and take action.

Setting boundaries

Prioritizing your focus is all about setting new boundaries. Once set, don't breach these boundaries. People will attempt to insert their own priorities into yours, disrupting your workflow. Resist the temptation to allow such breaches to occur. Be conscious that you are the guardian of your time and you decide how to spend it. If someone else reprioritizes your workflow and you allow it, then there's only one person to blame.

Setting boundaries and sticking to them requires a new level of self-discipline. Leaders who set the boundaries of their priorities and don't allow them to be crossed are conscious of the activities on which they spend their time.

When setting the boundaries of your priorities, examine three areas:

Yourself: Identify the benefits of maintaining your priorities. Remind yourself of what happens if you allow a breach of the boundaries you've established.

151

Other people: Anticipate those who will undoubtedly attempt to breach your established priorities and thereby disrupt your focus. Figure out how you'll respond. Sometimes they may have a good point, and when they do you can adjust your priorities to bring them into your workflow without disrupting your priorities.

Other intrusions: The most common are incoming emails. Then there's the unwanted, urgent telephone call. Third is the uninvited visitor. Emails are bothersome with the new technology of the email ghost. Some Outlook users have a small ghost that comes up in the lower right corner announcing the sender and subject of just-received emails. Resist the temptation to drop everything and respond to the email ghost.

If you don't want to take any telephone calls for a time, then either don't answer or simply unplug your telephone. Be sure to turn off your cell phone as well for those who are more persistent in interrupting your focus.

Uninvited guests are a problem because you don't want to be rude. Here's how to deal with someone who just shows up at your office door and insists on an audience: Stand up and grab their hand to shake and steer them toward the door. Be polite, but ask they send you a note suggesting a more convenient time to meet. Wish them good-bye, close your door and get back to work.

Micromanaging

This is one of the most disruptive and unnecessary enemies to working down your list of priorities. Many otherwise effective leaders spend a significant part of their days following up with subordinates, demanding overly frequent updates on progress and otherwise inserting themselves into tasks where they are unneeded and largely unwanted.

If you're a micromanager, stop it. Some newly promoted bosses, who are unsure how to do their new job, insist on still trying to do the job they once had. They do this by micromanaging their replacement. Because they were good at it and were sure of what to do, it gives them a false sense of security. Stop it.

One key to ceasing this micromanaging is to hire people whom you trust, who are better at their jobs than you are and who simply won't stand for your meddling. Why waste your time and theirs on unneeded and unwanted supervision? If your subordinates are fully engaged, they're sufficiently challenged and skilled enough to lose themselves in the work. Trust them to do what you hired them to do. Make it clear that your help and advice are always available if requested, otherwise they're on their own and you expect them to achieve the intended results. Then step away and get back to your own work.

The power of resilience

It doesn't matter how many times you fall. What matters is how many times you get back up. Getting back up is resilience. We can't control the cards we're dealt, but we can control the way we play them. Sooner or later we get exactly what we expect, whether we expect success or failure. Our expectations drive the ultimate outcome. The key to consistent success is the *expectation* of success.

For example, think of when you are training your dog. The successful trainers look their four-legged student right in the eye and give the command once with the expectation that it will be followed. This technique is far more successful than those weak sisters who *ask* the dog to do something but really don't expect success with just one request. Consequently, you hear them repeating and repeating the same command (and often others) until the poor dog is both bored and confused.

The expectation of success breeds success. If you aren't a natural optimist, you can cultivate the expectation of success by:

- Releasing your emotions—let those you lead get to know the real you and what makes you tick.
- Maintaining a positive, never say die, attitude as you work yourself and your team out of the inevitable problems that occur.
- See the solutions in every problem. Believe in yourself and your ability to succeed. Maintain your optimistic attitude.
- Handicaps—such as a lack of sufficient resources to complete a project—can only stop you if you let them. The real limitations reside only in your mind. Your creativity and perseverance can sweep them out of the way.

Is the past holding your life hostage?

The failure to succeed in one thing has a definite end. Find that end and move on. Don't keep beating yourself about what went wrong. Failure in one thing is just the door to succeeding in the next opportunity. Know that your next breakthrough is just around the corner. Here are the signs that your past is holding you hostage:

- Comparison of the current situation with past failures
- Offering excuses for a failure
- Isolating yourself and withdrawing after a failure
- Regret at failing. This just saps the strength that you'll need to succeed in the next opportunity
- Harboring bitterness. This is the consequence of failing to get over past injuries

If you see that your past might be holding your future hostage, begin with just two simple exercises. First, acknowledge the pain you're in, then remove it from your life. If necessary, forgive both yourself and others for their role in your past failure. Accomplishing these two things places you on the path toward succeeding.

Strengthening your resilience

Training yourself to bounce back from life's challenges is a learned skill. Most of the learning is about yourself and how you deal with adversity. Here are four techniques to strengthen your resilience:

- See yourself clearly, accepting your strengths as well as your weaknesses.
- Admit your flaws accurately and accept those things that you cannot do well. Then don't keep trying to master them.
- Develop your strengths so that you truly excel at those things you do best.
- Pursue your passion. Make it your central cause, purpose and *Why*. Do not imprison yourself in a job or profession in which you have no interest nor derive any pleasure or sense of accomplishment.

Lessons learned

America's space program taught us the value of failure. Each one—even the Apollo and space shuttle tragedies—were teaching moments. We succeeded because we weren't afraid to fail. Indeed, the most successful of us fail early and fail often. But from each failure we learn something valuable. The adversity that failure brings is simply a step toward eventual success.

The pain caused by failing has several benefits:

- Resilience and observing how tough you really are
- Maturity
- Falling, then getting up, then falling, and then getting up again is a process that extends your confidence in taking risks a little further each time. This process builds your resilience.
- It teaches innovation—you see what went wrong and can stop it before it happens again.
- Failure doesn't feel very good. Yet, it motivates success.

Edison—a world-class failure

Thomas Edison was a great inventor *because* he failed more often than he succeeded. He always learned from his mistakes. Eventually his relatively few successes far outstripped his many failures. Edison learned resilience.

Once a journalist challenged Edison by asking why he kept trying to make light using electricity when he has failed so many times. The journalist even postulated that gaslights are here to stay. Edison replied, "Don't you realize that I have not failed but have successfully discovered six thousand ways that won't work!"

Edison refused to give up. He tried countless materials in his search for a filament that would work. His men scoured China, Japan, South America, Asia, Jamaica, Ceylon and Burma in search of fibers that might glow when passed through by an electric current. Nothing worked. Then, on October 21, 1879, after thirteen months of failing, Edison asked himself, "Why not try a carbonized cotton fiber?"

It took going through two spools of cotton until he finally succeeded in placing a carbonized thread into a vacuum-sealed bulb. His laboratory lit up and the world had the light bulb—but only because of one man's resilience to failure.

Resilience toward risk

Nothing great ever comes from taking the safest route. Risk begets success. The bigger the risk, often the greater the reward. In baseball, swinging for the fences is a huge risk for the batter. However, the potential home run is the greatest reward.

Everything worthwhile carries its own risk. The quandary is whether that risk is worth the potential reward. The CEO's job usually entails balancing the risk with its potential reward without endangering the organization's cause, purpose and *Why*.

There are a number of traps to avoid when evaluating risk:

- The risk of embarrassment
- The rationalization trap: Trying to rationalize away the need to take this risk
- Unrealistic expectations versus the low probability of succeeding at such a high level. The answer then becomes, why even try.
- Timing: Now is not the best time, so we won't try. The fact is that there will never be a perfect time to do anything.
- Inspiration: You don't have to be great to take the risk, but you do have to take the risk to be great.

Finally, you can tell you're not taking enough risk when you succeed at everything you do. Extend yourself. Expand your goals. Move your targets down range a little more.

Resilience means getting up when you're knocked down

True, but it's more than that. What do you do once you've picked yourself up? First, failing is no fun. So you need a plan that stops you from continuing to fail. Here's how to do just that:

Identify your goal. The ultimate goal defines the actions needed to get there.
- Define your plan: Like a SCUBA diver, plan your work and work your plan. Anything else is a recipe for failure.
- Take action, accept the possibility of failure.
- Don't welcome mistakes, but recognize that you and your team will make them. Dissect each failure. Learn from each mistake. You'll build a body of knowledge that lessens repeat errors that lead to failure.
- Don't give up. Ever. In each risky endeavor there is always a defining moment when quitting is easier than persevering. Pass the moment and press on.
- Continually evaluate progress toward the goal. Make course corrections when needed. Adapt to the situation and change when necessary.

The power of the right habits

A Duke University research report in 2006 stated that 40 percent of the actions people perform each day arise from habits rather than from conscious decisions. Habits are learned behaviors that occur without you having to think about doing them. Develop the right habits that move you toward your cause, purpose and *Why*. Three ways that develop the right habits are:
- Identify your existing habits and stop them if they don't help.
- Define each habit that you want to develop. Visualize the behavior, outcome and actions inherent in that habit. Then practice it.
- Focus on small changes and wins rather than global changes in your habits.

Learning your keystone habits

These are the habits that matter the most to your success. They influence how you work, eat, play, live, spend, and communicate. Keystone habits don't depend on getting everything right. Instead they focus on a few priorities and fashion them into powerful levers.

Identifying keystone habits is tricky. To find them, look to the organization's culture. For example, say an enterprise has a culture that accepts berating and humiliation as a way to embarrass employees into doing their work. This may be fine for the Marine Corps, but it's probably not the way you want your organization to run.

Instead, you want a keystone habit that respects the experience, expertise and judgment of every employee. There is room for disagreement and discussion. However, it is also clear that there is just one boss. Changing the culture to create this keystone habit comes from the top of the organization. Those who begin practicing it, define it. It is a conscious decision to change behaviors. It usually doesn't take long for a new, acceptable keystone habit to filter down, and throughout the organization.

An example of an effective keystone habit is the way former Captain "Sulley" Sullenberger managed the cockpit of his US Airways jet. Communication, suggestion, discussion, decision and action all took place on Sulley's flight deck within a matter of seconds between pilot and copilot once they hit a flock of geese and lost all engines. This was their keystone habit. It occurred without having to think about it. As the jet approached the Hudson River, both pilot and copilot relied on their training as they prepared for a very risky water landing. Paramount in their actions was their keystone habits and all the other sub-habits they had adopted. The result was one of the few completely successful ditchings of an airliner ever.

In the case of Sullenberger, following habits yielded a huge success. However, that's not usually the case when changing keystone habits. Go for the small wins, celebrate them and then move on to the next change. For example, in football the linebacker would dearly love to know which way the receivers are going to run, each time, every time.

For them, the keystone habit might be to watch the receiver plant his foot when he enters the secondary. It's hard to fake direction with a foot plant. Now the linebacker knows which direction the receiver is going and can react accordingly. This small win for the linebacker can turn into a devastating game changer for the entire team. Along with the increased probability of pass interceptions, the rest of the team can pick up the keystone habit.

Changing habits

Everyone identifies and changes their habits differently. When I'm changing the cultural habits of the organizations I work with, we typically follow a five-step process:

- -dentify the habit sequence that needs changing.
- Isolate the inciting incident that kicks off the unwanted habit sequence—now you know when it is coming and what to expect.
- Determine what changes(s) you want to make in the sequence.
- Experiment with rewards for making the change. Determine which unwanted habit to replace with the reward.
- Keep repeating the correction/reward sequence until you get what you want.

Take the Alcoholics Anonymous program as an example. When an AA member thinks they want a drink, they call their sponsor.

They do this to substitute the feelings they get from alcohol with the feelings their sponsor gives them. They end up getting the same feeling but by using the target keystone habit sequence.

Staying out of your own way

There is an art to not becoming your own worst enemy. Many otherwise very smart people can't seem to get out of their own way. For entrepreneurs with all kinds of new and important ideas spinning through their heads, this is particularly frustrating.

We call this *entrepreneurial attention deficit disorder*. These smart, creative people don't seem to focus on completing one project before they're off to the next. Such behavior is like a child constantly chasing the next shiny object. For entrepreneurs this lack of completion capability can be devastating for their enterprise as well as their investors.

For everyone who recognizes the need to stay out of their own way, there are a few imperatives to follow. The first is that everyone needs to acknowledge and embrace change. Change is good. It is progressive and it improves the overall work product. Those who reject change are just getting in their own way. Yes, sticking to what you know rather than what you're familiar with keeps you comfortable. However, that's not how you achieve your cause, purpose and *Why*. Reaching any goal makes demands on everyone. Some say, that any time you become comfortable, complacency can creep in and suddenly you're stuck in the mud.

Another imperative to watch for is denial that any change is needed. For example, say that the organization absolutely needs to lay off some of its people. If the CEO faces this fact and makes the decision, he has recognized that a change is needed. He didn't allow his feelings to get in the way of the larger CPW.

Failing Forward

This is the habit of successful CEOs. Certainly they fail—most fail more often than they succeed. The difference is that their failures move them closer to the ultimate goal. They learn something from each one. Failure is not final. It is just one step on the path toward success.

Small thinkers tend to isolate a single event that didn't yield the desired result and label it and everything associated as a failure. They cannot see this single event in the context of the bigger picture.

Conversely, those who fall forward, study what happened, learn from it and try again—usually with better results.

Realities of failure

Everyone fails. There are some facts about failing that everyone needs to understand. Among them are the things that failure is not:

- Failure is not an event, but a process that is part of the journey to success.
- No one can completely avoid failure—it is a condition of being human. Sooner or later we all will fail at something.
- Failure is not objective. Only you can label your actions a failure.
- Failure is not the enemy of success. It takes failure (sometimes many) to achieve success.
- Failure is not irreversible.
- Failure is not a stigma or a permanent mark on your forehead.

Everyone reacts to a failure differently. Yet, there are three things those who fear failing experience:

- Analysis paralysis: They keep cycling through the analysis phase of a decision to avoid actions that might lead to failure.
- Procrastination: They simply avoid embarking on a risky project once the decision is made to proceed. This steals time and saps productivity
- Purposelessness: They develop a policy of inactivity in order to avoid the pain of making a mistake.

Eliminate the fear of failure

The fear of failure is wrapped in so many other emotions: Fear of embarrassment, fear of being fired, fear of being seen as less than perfect, and the list goes on. Get over it.

There is not much difference in the actions that cause success or failure.

Think of the action a professional golfer uses to hit a 300-yard drive. The club head is traveling at 112 mph when it hits the ball. Allowing for the spring off of the clubface and the compression of the golf ball itself, it reaches a velocity of 165 mph at launch. At this critical point the chances of success or failure become minute. If the club head turns just a few millimeters, the ball will hook or slice off course. Suddenly, what could have been a crowd-pleasing 300-yard drive right down the fairway center becomes a rookie shot in the shape of a rainbow that lands deep in the trees, just 200 yards down range. Indeed, most golfers will tell you that this is a game of minimizing mistakes rather than pressing successes.

Four steps to approaching success

Persistence is what overcomes the many failures that lead to success. Because nothing worth achieving comes easily, you must

[handwritten: × Need to have rewards for those performing]

cultivate the habit of tenacity and persistence. Make these steps to approaching success part of your keystone habits:

- Find your purpose, your CPW: Make it the fuel that powers your persistence toward a successful outcome.
- Work with those possessing a great desire for an outcome similar to your own.
- Don't be content with the status quo—this only leads to mediocrity.
- Eliminate excuses as an acceptable explanation for failure. Take complete responsibility and move on.
- Develop incentives that reward success.
- Cultivate a culture of determination. This will foster persistence toward success.

Attributes of successful leaders

The most admired and successful leaders have a few things in common. The first is that they know themselves very, very well. They have no blind spots where their skills and weaknesses are concerned. Most successful leaders have excellent people skills. Chief among them is that they are good listeners.

Leaders who get results have a positive attitude. Success is always attainable to them—at least that is what they truly believe. Their optimism is contagious. They also seek out assignments where their skills and experience are most likely to move the enterprise further toward achieving its full potential.

Leaders who lack focus are generally not very successful. However, those with a laser-like focus on the ultimate goals and those things that will get the organization there are in high demand. They have organized their priorities so that there is a logical progression toward achieving the goal.

A CEO's Secret Weapon

Good leaders have an unquestioned commitment to achieving the goal, to the enterprise, and most importantly to those who will make the goal of success a reality. These are flexible leaders. If one strategy doesn't work—no matter whose idea it is—they are open to trying something different, they "pivot". If that also fails, they will try something else.

The most successful leaders are patient. They are willing to wait for results and don't try cutting corners for the sake of short-term expediency. These are the leaders with a measure of talent. However, their talent is not what they rely on. Their hard work and self-discipline earned them a seat at the table. It is their work ethic that will make their leadership successful.

Finally, the most sought-after leaders are visionaries. They have a dream and know the path toward achieving it. Their dream is their cause, purpose and *Why*. Their work ethic and skill in obtaining other's commitment to their CPW is what will make that dream a reality.

* * *

[Handwritten note: Build it out — CI with all clients, consultants, vendors]

Chapter 10: Becoming the Leader Others Want to Follow

Every great CEO is above all else, a great leader. Each has that magnetism that gets others to buy into their goal and their strategy for getting there. Leaders who fail to develop a team to help them achieve their goals are just smart people with a vision but no way to execute. Here's how to become the leader others want to follow.

First, trust yourself

The only magical thing about being a leader is the unwavering belief and trust the leader has in herself. In fact, every attribute leaders ascribe to those they lead must first be true of them. For example, if you want to be trusted, you must first trust yourself, your judgment, your courage and your ability to take the correct action.

Along with personal confidence in themselves, great leaders have an unwavering faith in their cause, purpose and *Why*. Their CPW never changes. However, the way they ultimately get there will certainly change as events and the environment in which they work unfolds. Weak leaders who constantly change their goals generate little faith in their character and substance. People see them as jellyfish, moving in whatever direction the prevailing current takes them.

If a person is going to follow the vision of another, they must trust that the person knows where she's going. Her actions and behaviors are consistent with her vision. This builds confidence in her judgment. People see her core values as something they can latch on to without feeling they will disappear, leaving them stranded. Such trust requires behavior that is consistently aligned with the leader's CPW.

One problem facing so many leaders is an unclear understanding of the real challenges facing them. Operational plans, revenue and sales forecasts, cash flow shortfalls, HR compliance, and the magical bottom line all conspire to obscure what really challenges them. Certainly, each of these lesser issues is important. However, they're not the most important. What's most important is how you influence others. It takes confidence in your abilities to accept the challenge of leading others. When a leader makes a decision, he affects everyone in the company and possibly their families. This is a huge burden.

Courage

Courage is the quality of mind and spirit that enables one to face difficulty, danger and pain without fear. For most business leaders the dangers are linked with the fear of being wrong. Leaders who make too many wrong decisions are often not around very much longer. That's the danger and the fear.

Courageous leaders possess a clarity and awareness about the impact they have on those they lead. Great leaders respect this responsibility and treat each decision with the weight they hold in their hands. This impact is paramount in making any decision and accepting the consequences for the results. Allowing themselves to be held accountable is part of the courage great leaders have. Effective leaders have the courage to reveal personal core values and weaknesses to the team. In other words, they show their human side.

Two primary values to merge into your leadership style are authenticity and personal responsibility. These qualities bring you the greatest sense of courage. It takes courage to look yourself right in the eye and get clarity on your cause, purpose and *Why*. Getting such clarity requires introspection, emotional intelligence, and a sense of focus.

Leaders, who attempt to lead as if they are without fault and refuse to listen to criticism and suggestions, soon diminish their personal credibility. Such leaders who insist on mounting such a pedestal of perfection set themselves up for a bad fall. Soon those being led begin looking for cracks in their leader's armor. It usually doesn't take long to find. Once they do, it's a slippery slide down for the deposed leader.

It takes courage to say, "Follow me, I know the way." Yet this is exactly the trust that CEOs are requesting of their subordinates when launching the next business strategy. In exchange for giving a leader their trust, subordinates demand that you be clear about where you're headed and why they should follow you there. "Because I'm the boss and I say so," won't take you very far.

The best leaders have a deeply personal connection with their subordinates. They care about the consequences of taking the prescribed actions and their subordinates know it. Further, both leader and subordinate are deeply connected to the cause, purpose and *Why*—their CPW.

Consistency of the goal

Once a leader has buy-in of his CPW by subordinates, the goal never changes. To do so would impugn the leader's credibility and draw into question his judgment. Acceptance of the CPW is difficult to achieve. Once attained do not change it.

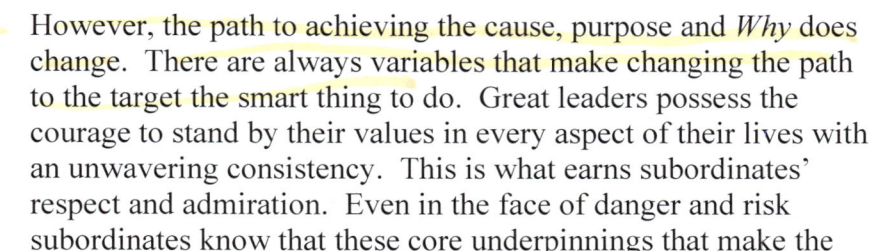

However, the path to achieving the cause, purpose and *Why* does change. There are always variables that make changing the path to the target the smart thing to do. Great leaders possess the courage to stand by their values in every aspect of their lives with an unwavering consistency. This is what earns subordinates' respect and admiration. Even in the face of danger and risk subordinates know that these core underpinnings that make the

A CEO's Secret Weapon

boss reliable will never change. Great leaders have this relentless commitment to achieving results with unyielding focus on their core values. Consistency of the goal is the great leader's way of life.

Action and inaction

We all solve problems by acting on information while using our best judgment. This is how we achieve goals and enjoy success. Conversely, those who waste time and energy on excuses and hesitation soon feel the emotional drain. Do not hesitate. Do not tolerate hesitation. Make your decision and then act on its implementation. Finally, don't second-guess your decisions.

To maintain the confidence of subordinates once a decision has been made, follow these three common sense actions:

- Keep talking with those impacted by the decision
- Update them on progress toward the target
- Maintain the team's commitment to the goal

Failing to act destroys the credibility of a leader faster than any other fault short of criminal activity. People who see a leader hesitate in using the power of his position soon conclude that the individual simply doesn't know what he's doing. They're right.

Here's a real life example of two fictitious business owners, Jeff and Jay, with a problem of inaction:

J&J AudioCorp. is 20 years old. Jeff and Jay have been partners since its inception. The audio/visual equipment sales division accounts for 70 percent of J&J's revenue—about $18 million annually. However, it contributes just 20 percent to the company's overall profitability. Jeff heads the equipment division.

Jay's Service division is much smaller revenue-wise than Equipment. However, he has created a profit and cash flow

169

machine. Service grosses just $7 million but is responsible for 80 percent of consolidated profits.

The 70 employees of J&J have noticed the conflict erupting between the two owners. Jay wants to shut down Equipment and concentrate on his vastly more profitable Service division. Had it not been for Jeff's indecisiveness in making this decision, Equipment would have been history some time ago.

I became involved when the two owners decided enough is enough and they needed a third party arbiter. It was quickly apparent that Jay was the visionary between the two. Jeff was afraid of upsetting the status quo and of leaving $18 million in gross revenue on the table if they shuttered Equipment.

Our analysis proved that the coming years would likely see Equipment becoming even less profitable than its present 1 percent margins. Their products were even now commodities. Sales were based solely on the lowest price. Further, using Equipment as a loss leader to get the vastly more lucrative service contracts of existing customers was economically ridiculous. Still, Jeff refused to budge. He was afraid of making the wrong decision and that it would be irreversible.

The first solution was to get Jeff and Jay to stop fighting. They needed to agree on their mutual purpose. It turned out to be the survival and eventual growth of the company. It didn't matter how, just that it happened and soon.

Obtaining their agreement was surprisingly easy. After all, these two had agreed on most everything for the last 20 years. Survival and growth was in the best interests of everyone—employees and their families included.

Next, they needed to show their team that both owners shared this unity of purpose and were no longer at war. We established a 30-

day timeline to make whatever decision they were going to make. We created a team to provide the research and forecasting needed to support this important decision. Everyone got to work.

By the end of that time, it was evident that the best decision was to sell the Equipment division to a strategic buyer. They would use part of the $45 million proceeds of the sale to invest in the Service division, expand it and create a brand name. The next day, they began interviewing investment bankers to do the sale.

Could Jeff and Jay have made this decision by themselves? Unlikely. The two had been wrestling with their dilemma for a year and had gotten nowhere. However, once they agreed on their singularity of purpose and were given the information they needed to make the decision, things became much easier.

The other benefit to eliminating their hesitancy came in the form of speed of implementation once they made that first big decision. They saw a window of opportunity open for the Service division that wouldn't stay open forever. Suddenly they had the money needed to capture significant market share. The rest is history.

Fear

As we just saw with Jeff, fear paralyzes. What to do? First, define the fear. Break it down into its component parts. For many organizations frozen by fear, people are afraid of being punished if they make the wrong decision. So, rather than take a risk of being fired, demoted or humiliated, they do nothing. At least there's no punishment for that. But there is a cost—often a huge cost for inaction. It takes on the form of missed market opportunities. IBM would have been a different company today had it not turned down a very young Bill Gates who wanted to sell them a license for his DOS operating system.

Corporate cultures that punish for wrong decisions create inaction. They stifle creativity and stop progress toward the ultimate goal.

Within such organizations, it takes real courage to make a decision and act in the face of such fear. Absent such courage, the risk-averse culture will affect other areas of life—especially for the CEO. Her public persona, health, relationships and attractiveness to new followers will soon wane.

Did you know that people are never afraid of taking action? It's true. Instead, they are afraid of the *result* if their actions prove wrong. In that sense, fear is a negative predictor of the future. So they take no action. Better the devil we know than the devil we don't.

Fear is governed by the ratio between perceived danger and confidence in the ability to cope with that danger. Those with high confidence can handle whatever comes their way, the fear they feel is minimized. These are the decision makers.

A simple way around this is to ask, *what would I do if I weren't afraid?* This takes away the risk of failure and isolates the action that you could take. Then you do the best with the information you have, trust your judgment and make the decision.

Managing the fear/confidence ratio

When the corporate culture stops subordinates, the easy thing to do is to tell them to make a decision anyway. However, that decision may well be influenced by their fear of consequences for being wrong and their ability to cope with that. When that happens, ask these six questions:

- What's the worst that could happen? What's the cost?
- What's the best thing that could happen? What are the profits?
- What's the most likely thing that will happen? What are the costs or profits?
- What's your plan if the worst happens?

- What's your plan if the best happens?
- What's you plan if the most likely thing happens?

Answers to these questions put a bracket around the costs and benefits of the decision. Often, when put in such an analytical construct, the worst scenario doesn't seem all that bad, especially if you already have a plan to deal with the worst consequences.

Be the Leader Others Want to Follow

You won't keep your rock stars by just giving them more money. Money is not a satisfier and its benefits don't last for very long. Then you're back to where you started, but with a more expensive employee. The most powerful form of leadership is the intrinsic motivation your subordinates feel within themselves.

CEOs with a visible, unshakable clarity and confidence in their cause, purpose and *Why* attract and keep the right people. These are the people who share the CPW. They follow the CEO because they believe what she believes. They follow *because they want to for themselves.* Here are six steps to generate such trust in your leadership:

Observable execution

These are actions that others can see and in which they can develop trust. They are actually watching to see if there's a disconnect between what the CEO *says* and what they're actually doing. This consistency between thought and deed goes a long way in instilling trust and respect. It says that you're still the same person, with the same CPW even when there's change for the worse.

Practice observable execution by executing one of the tactical steps in your business plan. Let everyone see how you manage change.

Personal warmth

People respect and follow those with whom they have a personal relationship. Those leaders exuding a personal warmth and who genuinely care about their people can get past the challenges of daily events. They have a personal stake in their people and vice versa. Everyone sees that behavior.

The best way to reach someone is to share your CPW. This is who you are and what you believe in. Such a personal sharing lets people into your life. They know something personal about you and feel they can now trust you.

Practice personal warmth by making it a point to ask your direct reports how they are doing. The stock answer when the boss asks such a question is, "Fine". Don't settle for that. Push a little and spend some extra time on each person. Then follow up on what you discovered. If they revealed a problem, see that it gets resolved.

Achieving clarity of purpose

Don't be afraid to be defined by what you want (your CPW) and what you expect. Be clear. Such clarity of purpose makes everyone more comfortable about their roles and responsibilities. People are far more likely to follow someone who knows what they want and where they're going.

To be sure you've done a good job in communicating your CPW, conduct a 360 CEO review. These reviews give the CEO a reality check. When conducted correctly they don't just give the good news. Actually, that's of less help than the things you're not doing right. Be sure to fix them promptly. Failure to do so will cause more damage than whatever positives the 360 Review may have created.

Buy into the vision.

If you've properly delivered an accurate clarity of purpose, people now have your vision. The next step is to get them to want to share that vision. People want to know that they're part of something much larger. Share that with them. Personal and emotional stories of your own CPW and vision help humanize the goal. People will judge for themselves. You want them to buy into your vision, not just the paycheck you're writing them every few weeks.

They say the best way to learn something—like a persuasive way of communicating your vision—is to write it, then say it. Continuously. Make your delivery credible, personal and convincing. Then ask them to buy into it.

Dealing with attraction and frustration

Good leaders have an almost magnetic attraction. They will attract the right people and only frustrate others. Identify those whom you want to attract to your cause, purpose and *Why*. Generally, the most substantive contributors to the mission are those with character and an integrity that runs deep. When faced with a choice, go with character over talent every time.

The Navy's Strike Fighter Tactics Instructor Program—Top Gun—creates the finest combat aviators in the world. Yet, aircraft piloting is just one of the attributes used in recruiting candidates for Top Gun. The Navy looks for character, integrity, team cohesiveness and the ability to teach others in its candidates for Top Gun. The reasons are simple: Raw talent without anything behind it dulls with age. Whereas, the person you truly are inside develops, gets deeper and smarter with age. Stick with character.

Reality

Things will go south. Don't let it bother you. Just press on. When you can deal effectively with the negative, people trust you. It takes much more to lead your way out of a storm than it does to navigate through calm waters on a clear day.

When things go wrong, as they inevitably will, don't assign blame. Instead, ask yourself what you did to cause the failure. Always begin with yourself.

I hope you have enjoyed reading, *A CEO's Secret Weapon* as much as I have writing it. The book incorporates much of what I have learned both as a CEO myself and as a confidante, guide and Special Lieutenant to countless CEOs. Learn these few simple techniques. Incorporate them into your daily routine. Become the leader that others want to follow. I wish you all the best in everything you do.

Frumi Rachel Barr, M.B.A., B.C.C., Ph.D.

About the author

Dr. Frumi Rachel Barr walks the talk. She has been the CEO of three enterprises and the CFO of two others. She has an MBA and a Ph.D. as well as multiple certifications in related specialties. She serves as personal confidante and coach to a number of high-profile CEOs. Dr. Barr is in the management trenches every working day.

Connect with me online

Twitter: https://twitter.com/Frumi

Facebook: http://www.facebook.com/Dr.Frumi

Linkedin: http://www.linkedin.com/in/frumirachelbarr

See My Products

100 Must Read Book Summaries: www.100MustReads.com

Stop My Email Pain: www.StopMyEmailPain.com

A final word from the author

It's still lonely at the top for some CEOs.

I began this book with the premise that it is "lonely at the top". During my research I was surprised to discover that a small cross section of CEOs aren't lonely at all. These are the ones in organized peer groups. However, the vast majority of CEOs are not in organized or even informal groups. It turns out they do feel isolated. They are open to joining a peer group. Only the distance and lengthy time commitment stop them.

Further, since publishing *A CEO's Secret Weapon* I've also found that two-thirds of CEOs do *not* receive coaching or leadership advice from outside consultants, coaches or their peers. I've also discovered that nearly all of these CEOs would welcome such a sounding board.

There is an answer serving both solutions

How to give this majority of isolated CEOs the peer support and resonance they need? The confluence of technology and demand have produced a completely new and innovative way to bring peers together. It is the Virtual Roundtable brought to you by The Frumi Group of Companies. Find out more at http://www.CEOVirtualRoundtables.com.

The book ends here, but a new chapter begins as I launch Virtual Roundtable as a new entrepreneurial adventure with a definite purpose. Virtual Roundtable creates a safe place for leaders to talk about what matters most. See how it aligns with your *Why*.

Read and study *A CEO's Secret Weapon*. Harness the personal power that comes from knowing your own cause, purpose and *Why*, then use the passion that comes with that knowledge to realize your organization's fullest potential. Don't wait another minute—your most complete success is just around the corner. Join a Virtual Roundtable to accelerate your success.

* * *

The Why Institute

Why Immersion

The Frumi Group has synthesized the best of the best practices and created the Why Immersion—an experience designed and customized for YOUR company. Inspired by authors Simon Sinek *(Start With Why)*, John Strelecky *(The Why Café)* and Oren Harrari *(Break from The Pack)*, Frumi adds her unique evolutionary touch to make a huge difference to your future.

Mission and vision statements are good things to have. But to break from the pack, a company would be wise to strive for something bigger than a mission and deeper than a vision. Consider going a step up, to a higher cause. A higher cause defines a noble and honorable purpose. A higher cause aims to leave a positive mark. It aims to change an entire market; in fact, it aims to change the world for the better. It's about somehow bettering the lot of human beings.

For your Customers: Higher causes focus on customers and potential customers: how they benefit and how their life or business will be elevated, all in a way that's fresh, compelling, unique, and, perhaps most important—uplifting and virtuous. The most powerful higher causes lead people to see how the world will be a better place, and how humanity will benefit anew.

For your Employees: A higher cause takes employees far beyond their career ambitions to feed their most profound ambition: to lead meaningful lives.

For your Company: A strong higher cause serves as an organization's strategic beacon, market brand, and organizational "soul". It drives all strategic and operational decisions. It demands collaborative excellence in performance. It pushes constant innovation in products and customer service. It spurs employees to continually reinvent and enhance the experience of customers.

It improves the odds of leaving a positive, lasting legacy in the industry and the world.

Our Pledge: The Frumi Group can guide you, and inspire you, the leader, to find YOUR cause, and then align it with your company's. Determining a higher cause is partly an analytical and intellectual exercise. You have to assess the external environment and your internal organization's capabilities, and you have to justify your decisions with economic logic.

Ultimately, a higher cause is almost a spiritual aspiration, one that is deeply felt and sacred in a secular way. A higher cause provides a deep personal purpose to you as a leader and to your colleagues, and it defines the deep purpose and persona, or soul, of your organization. When you as a leader can experience both analytical and spiritual elements as you determine future alternatives for your company, you're on your way toward defining a higher cause that will elevate your business to a new level.

Our "HOW": Please note that much of the forgoing was best said in Oren Harrari's book. Read more about the relevance of finding your coherent and authentic cause by reading the book notes from master synthesizer, Frumi Rachel Barr. You might also go to www.thewhyinstitute.com to read more about finding your "Why", your Cause.

In a nutshell: Imagine 3 days to get completely focused. In our 3-day intensive immersion with you we will facilitate the in-depth conversations that will allow your executive team to leave with tangible deliverables. All we ask of you is for 3 days of your time and your promise to be fully engaged with us and your teammates: no phones, no emails, and no interruptions. You will accomplish weeks' worth of work in 3 days. You will get results that are ready to be implemented and a corporate game plan that will allow you to return to the office and hit the ground running. If productivity in the work place jumps up 40% by doing just one team building activity, can you imagine how it would skyrocket by doing an entire "intensive" three days?

Not convinced? Read on…

The Secret to Success Starts With WHY
Every person and organization on earth knows what they do. Some even know how they do it…but very few know WHY they do what they do. Imagine if every organization started with WHY. Decisions would be simpler. Loyalties would be greater. Trust would be a common currency. If our leaders were diligent about starting with WHY, optimism would reign and innovation would thrive. Those leaders who inspire are not driven with what they do, they are driven by WHY they do it, their "cause". Gaining Clarity of Why is just a starting point to our WHY Immersion.

Once you know WHY, HOW will you bring your WHY to life?
HOW are the strategies, guiding principles, or values that inform the path you will take in pursuit of your WHY. They are the code of conduct to start to move a WHY into something useful. The actions you take or the environment in which you work best.

WHAT you do is HOW you bring your WHY to life. It is the products or the services that you offer. We offer a customized Immersion that fits your time and budgetary needs. Here are just a few outcomes that you can expect from your experience:

- --Clarity on what motivates each team member.
- --Clarity on how to leverage each team member's strengths.
- --The initiatives that you should be focusing on now.
- --An executable strategic plan.

WHERE:

We choose a venue that fits your budget and your starting location. Our goal is to offer you an exceptional experience.

AFTER the retreat:

- o --Follow up accountability teleconferences to ensure execution of action plans
- o --Individual coaching of the CEO and senior executive team
- o --Group and team coaching
- o --A multitude of seminars.

Simon Sinek, author of Start With WHY is part of our team – engage with us NOW! and experience an amazing acceleration in your business results.

Call now for your customized program! 949-729 – 1577 or visit www.thewhyinstitute.com

* * *

CEO Virtual Roundtables

CEO VIRTUAL ROUNDTABLES
Discussing what matters most!

As a CEO, President, or Business Owner...

Is This You?

- **You have a lot of responsibility** – your business thrives or dives depending on the decisions you make
- **You're tired of feeling like the buck** stops with you
- **You are ready to share the burden** with people you respect, trust and who are extraordinarily capable in their own right
- **You value** integrity, relationships and collaboration
- **You may have heard of CEO peer groups** – or even joined one – but you want a higher level of interaction and "just in time" CEO-to-CEO advice
- **If any of this rings true for you**, you are in the right place.

- **I've been there.** And the good news for you is that it no longer has to be that way...

Let's face it. Your business success depends upon...

- Your ability to identify **opportunities**
- Your capacity to make timely and appropriate **decisions**
- Your insight to detect **looming threats** on the horizon

Hard truth: Relying on your gut and personal experiences are not enough.

Imagine profiting from the experience and knowledge of other high-achieving
CEOs; from sharing and testing ideas with true peers from various industries and backgrounds who serve as your personal "board of advisors" in a safe environment that is built upon trust and accountability.

The CEO Virtual Roundtable Difference

- No all-day meetings
- No travel – everything happens at your computer
- Designed specifically around "CEO ADD" – no theory, no fluff, no excuses
- You decide who deserves a place on your CEO Team (just like the Navy Seals)

- 1-on-1's with your CEO Team Leader are on a "just-enough, just-in-time" basis
- Once a year, your group gathers in person to celebrate your successes

Email us now for more information at DrFrumi@CEOVirtualRoundtables.com (mailto:DrFrumi@CEOVirtualRoundtables.com) or click CEOVR Information (http://tinyurl.com/kp7knmj) for more details.

Still not sure?

Download **Are You Getting Value from Your Peer Group: Are You Ready To Participate** (http://tinyurl.com/m5l8kyr).

Apply Now

We invite you to join us. Please fill out your application (http://tinyurl.com/m4ej7rb) for the next CEO Virtual Roundtable. We'll be in touch to discuss your candidacy and if we feel we can add significant value to your business, we'll begin the process of matching you with the best group that is currently forming. Participate in the conversation – join the CEOVR LinkedIn Group now!

Made in the USA
Middletown, DE
19 October 2016